Voice Under
Every Palm

The author, Jane Reed, at ELWA mike.

Voice Under Every Palm

THE STORY OF RADIO STATION ELWA

by

JANE REED

and

JIM GRANT

ZONDERVAN PUBLISHING HOUSE
GRAND RAPIDS   MICHIGAN

266 023

There is a voice under every palm tree. All you need is a box to catch it. — Gio tribal comment concerning the miracle of radio.

FOREWORD

Radio is a significant symbol of the new strategy in missions today. It is new, but not a novelty. It is glamorous, perhaps, but not a gimmick. An ideal instrument for missionary propagation in Africa, radio goes a long way in providing solutions to the fourfold problem of manpower, multiplication, mobility, and maintenance.

Rising from the steaming jungle, ELWA's giant steel towers symbolize the hands of men and God joined in this great venture. The incessant pounding of the nearby ocean portrays the pulsating heart of God, as defined in the call-letter slogan Eternal Love Winning Africa.

With overflowing hearts we recognize God's goodness in using this instrument to bless Africa. From a tiny "palm kernel" beginning in 1954, ELWA has grown to a majestic "towering palm" today. Seventy missionaries and more than one hundred Liberians use its transmitters to reach all of Africa and parts of Europe, South America, and the Middle East, broadcasting hundreds of hours each week in forty-two languages.

Climbing the high walls of prejudice and opposition that isolate nations as well as individuals, ELWA speaks to the heart in the privacy of the home. Because of the prayer partnership of God's people around the world, ELWA links the hungry hearts of Africa's great peoples, however remote, with the One who said, "I am the living bread which came down from heaven."

Evangelism — the heart of ELWA's ministry — is coupled with Bible teaching for the strengthening of believers. Radio Bible School correspondence courses giving instruction in Bible subjects and training in effective Christian witness provide a means of growth to the emerging church.

The Sudan Interior Mission believes radio to be one of the most powerful instruments of this present day of missionary ministry. Together with literature, medicine, education, and other methods, it strengthens the hand of the soldier of the cross in the total effort to reach the multitudes. Missionary radio is a significant part of God's great plan to reach all of Africa with the Gospel. A tremendous challenge to this generation, it is a vital part of the entire effort of the church of Jesus Christ to "hasten the coming of the King."

In a book like this, which we trust will be a blessing to you, it is impossible to name all the people who have had a part in the establishment of Radio Station ELWA. They have nonetheless made significant contributions, and we give thanks to God for each one. In a very real sense, theirs, too, is part of the "voice under every palm tree."

RAYMOND J. DAVIS
SIM General Director

INTRODUCTION

I am happy to add this personal word of commendation concerning the ministry of ELWA. To my mind, this radio station constitutes the finest missionary outreach to the Continent of Africa, touching not only those in high government circles, countless numbers on lonely bush stations, but literally millions with the message of God's eternal love. Calvary Baptist Church is proud to be part of such a vital endeavor.

Hardly a week goes by without my receiving scores of letters from missionaries, Christian workers and nationals, telling of the benefit and blessing which "The Calvary Church Hour" affords each week. My heart is constantly stirred and challenged by the dedication and sacrifice of countless Christians who rise early each Sunday morning to receive spiritual food through our broadcast.

Only recently, a Nigerian, with tribal marks still evident on his face, came to me at the conclusion of one of my Sunday morning services. "Are you Stephen Olford?" he asked. After assuring him that I was, he said with deep emotion: "This is the day I have been waiting for, for such a long time." Conversation revealed that he had been a faithful listener to our broadcast over ELWA for many years, and the joy which he radiated was an evident token of the blessing which he had received. Such experiences could be multiplied a hundredfold.

It is my prayer that God will continue to prosper the ministry of ELWA and strengthen its voice at this crisis hour to proclaim the message of life and victory in Jesus Christ.

STEPHEN OLFORD
Pastor, Calvary Baptist Church,
New York City

CONTENTS

Foreword

Introduction

1. To Kill an Elephant

Powerful curtain array antennae system.

1. To Kill an Elephant

"'SCUSE, MR. REED. I come to tell you the people are coming!"
Robert stood nervously at the door for a moment, then disappeared
down the hall.

Dick Reed pushed back from his desk and stood. This was the
day. The big day. The pressure ripped little ragged edges around
his customary calm.

Outside, the distant beating of drums carried exciting news, and
through the palm fronds Dick could see the chattering Liberian
women in bright country dresses and men in colorful robes, all
hurrying to the road.

It had been an exciting week. An anniversary week. Radio
Station ELWA was ten years old. There had been ceremonies
and congratulations from every corner of the world. Liberia's
President Tubman had said, "Your religious and educational programs, news broadcasts and rich variety of public services these
past ten years have made ELWA's contribution to Liberia
invaluable."

Even as Dick stood, trying to gather the loose ends of his mount-
ing anticipation, four broadcasts were going out simultaneously!
English to Monrovia and vicinity; a vernacular broadcast for
Liberia's interior; French to Central Africa and the Congo; and
Arabic beamed to the Middle East. Four control rooms and four
transmitters were humming with busyness as usual.

Dick tightened his loosened tie and followed Robert down the

Village scene.

hallway. He smiled as he noticed the pride in Robert's walk, the unusual briskness in his step. And why not? This was Robert's day, too. His people were about to arrive.

As a child, Robert Grear had lived in a small pagan village in great fear of the massive Gedeh Mountains which surrounded him. He had watched as his people sacrificed white chickens at the foot of the mountains to placate the evil spirits.

While Robert was still young, a Liberian evangelist trekked long hours through the bush to his village, and told them of Jesus Christ. It was strange, this story about the true and living God, who loved the Krahn people. It was strange. And wonderful. And Robert was among the first to accept it as true.

Robert left his village and returned with the missionary to a mission school. And from the school, God brought Robert to ELWA. At ELWA, as Krahn Broadcast Director, he returned to his people, magically, from the little box that talked. They gathered under a palm tree or thatched shelter to hear their young man's voice, and, one by one, they were changed by what he told them. The evil spirits in the mountains were forgotten. The white chickens were no longer sacrificed. And a new building dominated the village — a church. A Christian church. And today, the Krahn Christians were walking the many miles to show their gratitude and to wish ELWA a happy birthday.

As Dick and Robert left the studio building, the sound and color were overpowering! The drums were closer and louder. Wide-eyed, laughing men, women, and children were running toward the road. At the entrance gate a band of more than sixty gaily dressed Krahn people, carrying "Happy Birthday" placards and waving palm fronds, jounced up and down to the insistent beat of the drums. Babies jogged contentedly on the backs of their mothers. Two elderly gentlemen in flowing robes led the procession with great dignity.

"What's that song they're singing?" Dick shouted to Robert over the noise.

"It says that many have come to our country, but have done small-small. ELWA has given us something."

"My home is too far a place to walk," added Robert's wife, Francis, flashing her usual, quick smile. She had joined them as they walked, and now looked wistfully at the shouting, singing visitors who had walked from their villages to ELWA.

"But the radio can go," Robert said.

By now people were spilling into the crowd from every direction. The grounds were a mass of Krahns, shouts, missionaries, back-pats, children, singing, hand-shakes, and laughter.

Dick and Robert called the Krahn people to the front, the others forming a circle around them. There was a sudden burst of approval as a blanket-draped creature pranced into the center of the ring.

"What's going on?" Dick asked.

"This is an elephant dance. It is used only for special times. In our country, the man who kills an elephant gets much honor and respect."

A second man entered the ring, cautiously pursuing the elephant. Every nerve taut, the hunter crept after the lumbering blanket. Slowly, melodramatically playing off the shouted encouragement of the crowd, the hunter stalked his prey. *Bang!* A perfect shot. The elephant stopped, swayed, and collapsed. The crowd was delirious with pleasure!

"The elephant is killed," Robert shouted in Dick's ear. "That means ELWA has won the victory. And now it is time for big feast!"

The pantomime continued as three Krahn women entered the circle and began "cooking" in great pots, surrounded by fascinated on-lookers. "Cooking" completed, the oldest woman rose from her crouched position. Sophie de la Haye (wife of ELWA's manager) was pushed into the circle, her light laugh in sharp contrast to the mock-seriousness of the women at the pots. The old woman walked to Sophie and presented to her the utensils used in the cooking.

"When the women give pots and pepper board to the wife of one of the big men, that means the women share in the victory by cooking the chop for feast."

Sophie seemed to sense the meaning Robert was explaining to Dick, and her obvious appreciation was cheered by the happy crowd. Dick sensed a depth to the noise that might not have been observed by the superficial observer. These Krahn believers had come so far, and were now so pleased to do anything which would convey their thanks. The little box that brought their Robert's voice to them had also brought them new life. And here was the place it all started.

One of the robed gentlemen who had led the procession stepped forward. Ray de la Haye was summoned with a grand gesture.

Robert whispered, "That's the Senator from our district. He was one of the first in our town to find Christ. He was beaten and driven from his own town. He knows what it is to suffer for Christ."

The story was left unfinished as the Senator offered a parcel to Ray. With his usual precision, Ray carefully unwrapped it, saving the string, and then held it high, for all to see — a bright African painting.

Robert's voice trembled with pride. "That is a painting of our village at the foot of the Gedeh Mountains. The people around the radio under the tree, those are my own Krahn people. They listen to ELWA!"

"With this small something," the Senator intoned carefully, "all the Krahn people want to say 'thank you' to ELWA." His gesture swept across the throng of smiling Krahns. "We want to say that we are always listening to ELWA. You have given us Christ and a new way of life, and we say 'thank you plenty!' "

As another cheer subsided, Ray raised his hands for attention. "We are grateful, too. We are grateful that God has brought us here to serve Him. And we are grateful for what is happening in your hearts and the hearts of many across Africa. But we are only His tools. God, not ELWA, deserves all the glory. Thank you for this token of your thanks and love. God bless you."

Then Dick Reed stepped forward to speak. "This station could not be handled alone," he said. "This is why we have brought young men like Robert to represent the many languages in Liberia. We're working together. We come from many different countries. We are many different colors. But we are all one in Jesus Christ."

Time disappeared, and soon the benediction was given, and the Krahn people again broke into their rousing victory song. The drum called them into formation, and they began to leave as they had come. The children, the missionaries, the staff, and the visitors began to drift off to their various homes and duties.

Dick sat on the railing of the studio porch, watching the last of the visitors retreat into the twilight. Jane joined him, and together they watched the last stragglers become silhouettes against the deepening red sky.

A whimsical look crossed Jane's face. "Know what this reminds me of?" she asked.

"I think so," Dick answered quietly. "That evening twelve years ago when we first came to Liberia. It was a twilight like this."

Jane smiled, the memory filling her with satisfaction. "Only six of us then. Now we are more than sixty. It's wonderful what God has done."

Dick didn't answer. No words were needed. They sat until after dark, the night surrounding the peaked roof of the hospital, the schoolhouse, the transmitter-generator building, the staff houses, and the dozens of antennae reaching up. It was so much. And it had started so small.

2. "Wait Small"

2. "Wait Small"

"THREE STUDENTS TO TALK about radio for Africa," read the note on Dr. Edman's appointment pad. In all his years as president of Wheaton College, he never remembered being quite so curious about an appointment.

The office buzzer announced the mysterious three. Dr. Edman rose to welcome them. Outside, students scurried between classes in the crisp early spring air.

"Bill Watkins, Merle Steeley, and Abe Thiessen to see you."

Dr. Edman smiled and considered the three standing before him. He had seen them on campus: Bill Watkins was a night watchman, Merle Steeley worked in maintenance, and Abe Thiessen managed the campus craft shop. "So you're interested in radio for Africa," he said as they shook hands. "Have a seat, and tell me what's on your minds."

The meeting was short and to the point. The three were convinced that God was leading them to establish a radio station somewhere in Africa. "A small group of students here on campus has been praying for many months, asking God for direction. He indicated we should come and talk with you."

Dr. Edman assessed the seriousness and commitment of the group. Finally he asked, "Do you have any organization formed yet?"

The boys looked at each other. "Nothing official, if that's what you mean."

"What about resources? Do you have a mailing list of friends that you are keeping informed about this possible project?"

The boys looked down. "No."

"What about contacts? Do you have any contacts in Africa which could help direct your thinking as to where such a station could be located?"

The weight of all that they didn't have pressed the boys' spirits down. "Now you see why we've come to you."

Dr. Edman smiled. They were all aware of the size of the dream, now. He suggested that an official group be formed, that contact with established missions in Africa be made, and that a mailing list be formed to begin telling Christians what was happening. Then Dr. Edman opened the well-worn Bible on his desk, and read, "Fear not, O land, and be glad and rejoice; for the Lord will do great things."

There was a new look shared by the three as they knelt with Dr. Edman to pray. Before it had been the brightness of a dream; now the expression had deepened to that of dedication. The task was clearer. But God was shomehow greater because He had given them an impossible task to perform.

After the office door closed, and Dr. Edman was left alone, he buzzed his secretary. "I'd like to be alone for awhile. Re-schedule my next appointment."

He knelt again by his chair. "Dear Lord," he prayed, "give me the faith of these young lads. They are setting out on a tremendous project with no human resources in view. Guide us, and show us that this vision is from You."

* * * * *

"It's here! It just came in this afternoon's mail! It's here!" An excited group pressed around Bill Watkins as he displayed the official papers for which they had been waiting.

"Incorporated in the State of Illinois," Abe Thiessen announced. "The West Africa Broadcasting Association. W. A. B. A. Sounds good, doesn't it?" The happy chatter from newly formed "WABA" made it unanimous!

Following Dr. Edman's suggestions, a mailing list was being completed. There was much activity as "WABA" was attempting to make itself known. But, as they worked, they were aware that they were no closer to Africa than when they had begun.

Then, one night, a visitor appeared at the WABA meeting. Norma Bloomquist, a former Lutheran missionary and now serving as Director of Literacy in Liberia, was curious about this unusual prayer group. Before the evening was over, Norma spoke out. "Come to Liberia. It's one of the two independent countries where such a radio station would be possible. President Tubman is a personal friend of mine, and when I return to Liberia, I'll try to pave the way."

Norma returned to Liberia from her summer classes. The months dragged by. The hope she had brought them began to cool as the snow swirled around Wheaton College's old tower. Then it happened!

"Well, what do you know!" Bill shouted, not caring who heard. "Well, what do you know!" It was there in the WABA mailbox, short and sweet. "SEND MAN. DISCUSS TERMS OF FRANCHISE. Signed PRESIDENT WILLIAM V. S. TUBMAN."

❉   ❉   ❉   ❉   ❉

Less than one month after the invitation arrived, Bill Watkins and Norma Bloomquist were ushered into President Tubman's office at the Executive Mansion in Monrovia. This was a big day. The WABA group would be praying. Bill knew that. And they would be waiting for the answer — the starting signal for the radio station.

Conversation came easy with this warmhearted African leader. Briefly Bill explained the whole project. The President listened carefully, then sat back. To Bill it seemed a long time before he spoke again.

"We're interested," he said, "but we aren't ready just now for this project. Come back next year. Perhaps we'll be able to talk then."

Bill Watkins could hardly believe what he had heard. Had God sent him all the way to Liberia for this? The interview was over. The pair found themselves outside the Mansion before either could find words.

"I'm sorry, Bill," Norma said, feeling a bit guilty herself. "I really am sorry. But working with the President as long as I have . . . well, once he says 'no,' he means it. Come back next year as he suggested. I'm sure he'll give you the answer you want then."

Come back next year? No one knew how the tiny WABA group had scraped to finance this trip. They had put all their hopes, and every available cent into it. And now he was being told, "Come back next year." If there was to be a next year for the group, God had to do something *now!*

And so he began the long, fruitless round of visiting government offices. A political convention in Monrovia was keeping all offices in a constant busyness; visiting dignitaries, officials, guests and hangers-on, trooped in and out, day and night. Bill was hardly noticed. And his request to talk about establishing a radio station was so remote from the considerations at hand that it hardly rated a look.

Each evening Bill returned exhausted to his room provided by a small mission group. The house, sitting high on a stone foundation, overlooked the main shopping district. Off in the distance was Providence Island where the first pioneers, freed slaves from America, had landed many years before.

Just below the open window, the din of vendors, children, barking dogs, and honking horns had at first seemed wild and penetrating. Now they formed a slurred, frustrated background for his thoughts.

An occasional letter from his wife, Grace, said, "We're all praying," but Bill's mood lowered as he thought of what seemed the inevitable outcome of his trip.

When he could command the attention of some official or secretary, Bill was always told to see the Postmaster General. He was the one who could issue a permit, if anyone could. But always, Bill's visits resulted in long hours of sitting, waiting, mopping the perspiration from his brow and forearms, and waiting some more, while an equally uncomfortable secretary injected an occasional, "He'll be coming just now. Wait small."

"If you really want to see this man," the secretary finally said as she was closing her desk for siesta one day, "you'd better catch him in his own house, early in the morning."

Early the next morning, Bill walked through the sleeping streets of Monrovia to the gray zinc home of the Honorable McKinley A. DeShield. The immense structure, with a front piazza facing the street, was set just off the sidewalk. The wooden shutters were still tight across the windows.

There was no sound from inside the house, and Bill's knock

was less firm than his purpose. There was a long pause, and then the door opened a crack. One bright eye peered out, and then the door opened wider. A little Liberian girl, surprised at the light-skinned visitor, stared at Bill.

"May I please see the Postmaster General?" Bill asked, taking a quick survey of the room beyond the half-opened door. "It's very important."

"There's no way," the little girl answered, as though this were a memorized speech prepared for every intruder. "He's taking chop just now."

The clink of a cup and saucer in the next room touched a chord of desperation in Bill. The man he needed to see was just beyond reach. Without another word, he pushed past the startled little girl, and walked toward the dining room.

He stood silently in the doorway, studying the massive form of the man, still in his bathrobe, leaning over the table. In one hand, the Postmaster absent-mindedly held a cup of coffee. His attention, however, was fixed on the papers spread out before him.

Bill stepped quietly behind him. The little girl watched from the doorway. The Postmaster was so engrossed that he was unaware of his visitor.

It was a surveyor's map of property that was spread out on the table. Bill looked at it and remembered many summers spent with a survey crew in North Carolina. Then, to his surprise, Bill noticed a mistake in the drawings. Impulsively, he reached out, and followed the surveyor's line of error with his finger. "Excuse me, sir, but isn't this a mistake?"

"Where?" mumbled the Postmaster without looking up.

"Right here, sir. If you'll add up those angles, you'll see they don't agree."

The Postmaster did add the angles, and they didn't agree. "You're right! That's the mistake I've been looking for."

It was simple. It was miraculous. The official had been surprised to find a complete stranger looking over his shoulder at his breakfast table, but pointing out the error opened the door to friendship. It didn't take Bill long to lay out the hopes of WABA. The following day, when Bill arrived at the Postmaster General's office, there was no long wait.

Together they worked out the aims of the West Africa Broadcasting Association, ". . . to be established for the purpose of

propagating the tenets of the Christian faith as found in the Holy
Bible by means of radio broadcasting."

Exhausted, but rejoicing, Bill winged his way back to Wheaton
with the unofficial copy of the broadcast permit in his briefcase.
The official copy with the signature of the Commissioner of Com-
munications would be in the mail soon.

3. WABA, ELWA, and SIM

3. WABA, ELWA, and SIM

IT WAS LATE AFTERNOON, the first week in November, 1952. All day the sky overhead had been clear as the freighter, *African Pilot*, plowed its way through a calm Atlantic toward Africa's west coast of Liberia.

The monotonous churning of the motor and the easy roll of the ship made it impossible for Dick Reed, stretched out in a canvas chair, to keep his eyes open. The extravagant leisure was rare, and Dick soaked it up even more than the warm sun. Tomorrow, if the schedule was kept, this would be an indulgent memory.

His half-doze seemed to smooth the rough spots of the last two years. Yielding to the hypnosis of the rolling ship, Dick allowed the pictures to file by.

He and Jane had joined the little WABA group at the time Bill returned with the permit. Strange, God's leading, beginning back so many years before that. Growing up in the parsonage in Streator, Illinois. Meeting missionaries in the church from around the world. Navy days spent in the Philippines and Japan, seeing first-hand the spiritual need. The need, the tremendous need — that had left an indelible impression. Wheaton College, radio experience, all God's preparation.

During the summer on Jack Wyrtzen's Word of Life Camp staff, an important piece fit in the picture. Dick met Jane, from Chillicothe, Ohio, six months old in the Lord. It was hard to believe that she had spent eighteen years in Sunday school and church without once hearing the truth. "But the first time I heard Christ died for me," she had said, "I believed it."

The next summer they were at camp — as husband and wife. 1949 was an important year for them. Traveling with Jack Wyrtzen. Bible school for Jane, then the final year at Wheaton College. And all the while trying to determine God's place of service. Even with the preliminary applications to two missionary radio stations, God was saying, "Wait."

Then WABA came into the picture. Bill's report on Liberia held special fascination. "We have the most liberal permits in the history of missionary radio," he had explained. "It is a gigantic task and a gigantic opportunity."

Soon Dick and Jane found themselves not only praying with the WABA group, but helping with mailings and meetings on weekends. Before any of them were aware of it, the school year was over, graduation was past, and they were faced with life-determining decisions.

Packing to move from their apartment to Northwestern University for Dick's summer classes in radio, Jane found a set of application papers to a radio station they had been interested in. "Look what I found!" she exclaimed. The papers had never been sent. Somehow they had found their way to the bottom of a desk drawer. "What are we going to do about these?"

"I guess we've *already* done something about them," Dick smiled, flattening the creases that the papers had accumulated in their travels.

"You mean, by doing nothing, we've done something?"

"We've prayed for months, 'Lord, where in the world will You have us go?' We've looked all around the world. And He's shown us His place right here, in our own back yard!"

Jane looked dubious. "But I always thought God's direction would be more dramatic than that. No lights flashing? No mysterious call? Just . . . well, just here we are?"

"God has opened the door, and we've walked right into the middle of everything! It all fits! We're on our way to Liberia!"

That was two years ago. Back on ship a passer-by threw a momentary shadow across Dick. He looked up, but the bright sun obscured any clear image. He closed his eyes again.

There had been shadows across the WABA progress, too. They had tried to find a mission society which would be interested in the radio project in Liberia. But they found only missions already involved in their own expansion projects, and not ready to consider a venture the size of WABA.

Although the group had been busy with full schedules of meetings, churches had been cautious. Funds came slowly. And there had been the inevitable advice from a well-meaning Christian brother, telling them to forget their new-fangled idea and get out and preach like men.

But there were others, like Dr. A. D. Helser of the Sudan Interior Mission, who bolstered their spirits. His advice was simple. "If your vision for radio in Africa is from the Lord, don't let anyone or anything turn you aside."

It had been late September, 1951, when Abe called an emergency WABA meeting. The grand total of their treasury, he informed them, was just over twenty-five hundred dollars, hardly enough to get one of them to Liberia, let alone begin work on an actual facility. God would have to work a miracle. They all agreed to that. Their growing impatience and seemingly fruitless activities had to be resolved.

And so they prayed. And prayed with finality. The tone of the prayers was no longer, "Show us what we must do," but it was, "We've done all we know and can. Now, Lord, You do it!"

In a simple step of faith, the little group sent Bill Watkins to Liberia in November. At last there was action that looked like progress.

In Liberia, life and progress were not simple or fast, but the praying group back home made a difference. It had been no accident, finding the fishing settlement of King Grey near the ocean. The villagers listened to Bill preach that Sunday, but he couldn't take his eyes from the long strip of unclaimed land stretching along the ocean. The water in front, Monrovia just twelve miles away. It seemed perfect.

During this time the Sudan Interior Mission had expressed cautious interest. C. Gordon Beacham, S.I.M. Field Director in Nigeria, saw definite potential in the proposed station. He also realized young Bill in Africa could profit by encouragement and help.

Bill, in Liberia, was soon joined by Mr. Beacham from Nigeria, and an S.I.M. technician from Ethiopia. Together the three finalized the choice of land: 180 acres of tribal reserve released

by King Grey Village. Within a few months the arrangements
were settled. Soon a land grant would be considered.

The West Africa Broadcasting Association was now, thanks to
the indisputable help of God, ready to begin its work!

Things happened quickly from that point on. Duty-free privi-
leges were granted by the Liberian Government, allowing expensive
equipment to enter the country without extra expense. A frequency
was assigned, 710 kilocycles, and the call letters ELWA were
designated. ELWA: Eternal Love Winning Africa. Yes, all agreed.
That motto — those call letters said it. Radio station ELWA was
becoming less of a vision, and more of a reality!

Reluctantly, Dick let himself be aroused from his reverie by the
shuffling feet and scraping chairs near him. He blinked in the
dazzling light. Jane and their Liberian traveling companion,
Mrs. Elizabeth Collins, wife of the Liberian Assistant Secretary
of Interior, were settling into their deck chairs.

"Where have you two been?" Dick asked, shaking his mind
loose from the last few minutes.

"We went into town to do some shopping," Jane quipped. "No,
really Mrs. Collins is giving me a wealth of information about
Liberia. I knew the country had become independent in 1847,
but I had no idea of the hardships of the first pioneers who
arrived from the States back in 1822."

"Our forefathers came as slaves from the deep South in America," Mrs. Collins said. She had a small, proud smile. "Liberia
was to them the fulfillment of their dreams — a land of freedom
where the cross of Christ could be planted."

"The country has come a long way," Dick reflected. "How
common are radios?"

"It's hard to say. The interior is a long way from the capital
city of Monrovia. In the city, radios are common, but in the
hinterland . . . it's hard to say."

Mrs. Collins continued filling Dick and Jane in on the country
which was to be their new home. The people were friendly. English was the official language. "Although," she injected, "there are
twenty-eight Liberian dialects spoken throughout the country.
Broadcasts in these local dialects could do a great deal to unify
the country."

Many missions had established schools and churches in Liberia,
due mainly, to the encouragement of Liberia's President Tubman.

His background in a Christian home and training at the Methodist Mission school made him a strong church layman and sympathetic to the cause of Christ.

"Will you be making use of government subsidies to operate your radio station?" Mrs. Collins asked.

Dick explained that the West African Broadcasting Association had recently merged with an interdenominational faith mission, the Sudan Interior Mission. The money to finance the operation would be coming from God's people all over the world, channeled through the offices of the SIM.

Mrs. Collins and Jane began talking about the shops in Monrovia, the climate, and the food. Dick closed his eyes again. His mind traveled back to the merger with the SIM.

Full of apprehension, he and Abe Thiessen had gone to Toronto to meet with SIM leaders. The SIM had talked about radio for Africa many years before, when Dr. Rowland Bingham, founder and then General Director, was talking and praying for it. But efforts along these lines had been small and fruitless.

Now the interest of SIM leaders mounted as they talked with Dick and Abe about the project they had been negotiating for months.

Dr. Darroch, the Home Director for the mission, could see the potential of ELWA. The council agreed. The merger of the West African Broadcasting Association and the Sudan Interior Mission was made official.

Final organization was accomplished, but there was one disappointment. Abe Thiessen and his wife, Ellen, would not be able to go to Africa. Ellen's health wouldn't take the move. The little group had worked so closely together and seen such accomplishments, it seemed impossible that they would not all be together in Liberia. But so was the will of God, and so they accepted it.

Abe and Ellen would provide ELWA's home base, carrying the responsibility of promoting, recruiting, and financing the project. They would be working together . . . on opposite sides of the world.

The tinkle of ice cubes in a glass brought Dick's attention back to the top deck of the freighter. Jane and Mrs. Collins were talking about the rainy season. More than 200 inches of rain fell in six months . . . every year.

The rainy season. It had already affected ELWA's progress. Bush cutting had to be stopped, the road was washed out, the bridge collapsed, the road back to Monrovia was almost impassable, and the small farmhouse in which the few ELWA workers were housed had sprouted unnumbered leaks. Bill Watkins referred to this time of year as, "Mud, sweat and tears!"

Dick smiled as he remembered the two major sources of trouble: Rain and rogues. Rogues — funny word. But hardly a funny situation. The Steeley's glasses, watches, and flashlights, the Watkins' belongings, all wrapped up in a blanket had been carried away in the middle of the night by an unknown visitor.

Dick looked out at the bleak stretch of ocean. ELWA had come a long way, but it hadn't really even started. Rogues, twenty-eight languages, a mixture of Christianity, paganism and Islam, 200 inches of rain . . . Dick sighed. It would be a new life, all right. And an interesting one.

4. Of Rogues and Rats

4. Of Rogues and Rats

IN THE AFRICAN DUSK the "Green Hornet" skillfully slid between washed out ruts and potholes, carrying the Reeds toward their new home. Bill Watkins was at the wheel of the weathered green jeep, bouncing from topic to topic almost as fast as he was driving.

Hugging the road on each side were tall palm trees and tropical foliage. Now and then a small clearing revealed a neat village with thatch and mud houses straggling down to the ocean's edge. The red twilight made a strangely beautiful silhouette of the huts and people. Thin trails of smoke rose from flickering fires.

"Life will be easier if you learn two things right from the beginning," Bill was saying. "Patience and humor. There's no way to do anything fast. The African's way is to 'take time.' And nothing you can do will change things. And if you can't do anything about it, you'd better have a good laugh and start over.

"I didn't realize until we were here for a while," Bill went on, "what an opportune time God has given us to start. Liberia's younger generation is losing faith with the old superstitions. They respect modern ways and means. They have a decided void where their old beliefs once reigned. What a time for Jesus Christ to step in!"

The jeep swerved off the Big Road onto a bumpier side lane. It came to a stop before a massive corrugated zinc structure looming out of the shadows. "Welcome to Harris Farm," Bill announced grandly. "I hope you appreciate all its modern amenities."

The rickety three-story house, built on cement pillars, stood forlorn and neglected-looking in a maze of foliage. Windows were everywhere, banked on either side by crude wooden shutters.

Grace Watkins and Vera Mae Steeley were waiting at the top of the cement steps with kerosene lanterns. Soon the re-united six were chattering in the lamplight, sharing God's working on both sides of the water.

So many things had happened. One of the highlights had taken place at Maranatha Bible Conference in Michigan. After hearing Abe's presentation, the conference had delivered $6,500.00 to ELWA — enough to underwrite the first studio building.

A much-needed carryall was coming with the Reeds' loads. This would help transport building materials from the city to the radio site.

The staff, an RCA-trained technician, Herschel Ries and his wife, Sammie, both from Houghton College, had joined ELWA.

Their enthusiastic chatter was accompanied by weird shadows cast by the lamps, dancing across the rough plank walls, and the songs of the frogs from the surrounding swamp.

"We'll go over to the ELWA site first thing tomorrow," Merle finally said. "Right now, you two had better get settled in."

"Just a few more minutes," Jane said, as she read the last of the letters friends had sent ahead to greet them. Already the distance between them and home seemed unbelievably great.

"Sleep light, and listen," Grace warned. "We had a rogue a few weeks ago."

"And if you hear thumping in the walls," Bill added, "don't let it bother you. It's just the rats. They can't get out."

Dick and Jane followed Grace over the creaking floors to their bedroom at the far end of the house.

"You'll get a kick out of our houseboy, Sumo, when he sweeps the floors tomorrow," Grace said. "He just sweeps the sand into the wide cracks. There's no trick to housekeeping out here."

Left alone in their bedroom with one small lamp, Dick and Jane looked around at the furnishings. The bed, a small table, a wash basin — that was all.

"Look!" Jane exclaimed, "there's no glass in the window, no hook on the screen, no nothing! Sleep lightly! Who's going to sleep at *all?*"

"Where are you going?" Dick called as Jane took their only source of light and ran from the room.

"I'll be right back!" And she was, with an armful of empty tin cans. She set to work, constructing a booby trap on the inside windowsill. An occasional slip of her hand gave them a sampling of the clatter an unwanted visitor would set off.

After the light was blown out they lay quietly in the lumpy bed sensing the African night. The ancient house seemed to be swaying in the breeze.

With a start, they both sat up! A quick, light scampering sound filled the room. It came from the walls. The rats were performing as announced.

＊　　＊　　＊　　＊　　＊

Early the next morning they all piled into the jeep and jostled over the road toward the ELWA site.

"Here's the road we built. It took picks and cutlasses, and wheelbarrows to carry the rubble away, but we made it. It's just been opened all the way this month."

Dick, Bill, and Merle were standing at the mouth of the narrow, hand-carved passageway cut through the dense jungle foliage, just wide enough for the jeep to pass through. They drove over the places Dick had only read about in letters. The Sandy Flats that washed out during the rainy reason, the plank bridge that had disappeared under the rains. From across the ocean it had been hard to understand why this three-mile stretch took nine months to complete. But seeing it was all the explanation needed.

Bill stopped the jeep. "This is where we actually enter ELWA property. Center Avenue, that strip there, leads straight through our property and to the ocean."

They stopped again at the end of "Center Avenue." Tropical foliage grew green and thick to the sand's edge. The beach extended as far as eye could see. At each end of the property, a fresh water lagoon bubbled around jutting rocks. The three men looked at each other, and then at God's provision. This was the start, the tangible answer to their prayers from the living God!

＊　　＊　　＊　　＊　　＊

"Help! Come quick!" Jane's screams echoed through the old house.

The jungle . . .

Clearing the jungle . . .

. . . with hand labor.

Three miles of road by hand!

Our first road to ELWA's site — built by hand.

Dick grabbed the lantern and ran down the hall. With a shove of his shoulder he pushed open the bedroom door.

"Quick! They're everywhere! They're biting me!"

Dick held the lantern close to the floor. The light caught a narrow black line moving across the room, disorganized only at Jane's feet.

"Hey, they're ants!" Dick exclaimed. He gave a quick jump and brought a squirming ant from under his shirt collar.

By this time the rest of the household had thundered down the hall to the Reed's room.

"I don't think it's funny," Jane shouted, skipping around the room. "Where are they going?"

"They're driver ants," Bill said. "They're just welcoming you the way they've welcomed all of us. They're looking for food. And they'll find it, even though they're totally blind. These little creatures will eat every living creature they come across!"

Jane shrieked again. "This is no time for a zoology lesson! Do something!"

"When they file through a village," Bill continued, "they eat poultry, pets, even . . . well, anything they find. And when they leave, they leave nothing."

"You mean we just have to stand back and be eaten alive?"

"No, we won't give up that easily," Bill smiled. "But actually if they aren't in the way too much, it's best to let them clean house for you. But since it's bedtime, we'll try to divert their direction."

A short while later, with boiling water splashed around inside the house, and trails of gasoline set aflame in the yard, the driver ants finally retreated. After all the frantic activity, not even the thought of rogues, the heat, nor the tag-playing rats in the walls kept out a good night's sleep.

A cement block home near Monrovia had been offered to the Reeds by another mission. The home had served as a vacation house, but was now vacant. It appealed to Jane. There were no rats.

A series of bumpy rides from Harris Farm to the cement block house, the carrying of boxes and crates under the eyes of a curious group of Liberians who seemed to come up through the ground from nowhere, and they were moved in.

"The sun's almost down," Jane said with a shiver. "Night comes so quickly. The sun goes down, and presto! it's pitch dark." She paused a moment, pointing to the wall.

"What are you doing?" Dick asked.

"Shhh! Counting. Twenty-two, twenty-three, twenty-four! Do you realize we have twenty-four windows in four rooms?"

"Yep," Dick replied. "That's an awful lot of booby traps!"

Soon, the full African moon had risen, washing with milky light the sand stretching down to the ocean's edge. The whole panorama lay before them, the deep African night sky above. "It's almost a shame to sleep through all this beauty," Dick whispered.

"Yes," Jane agreed, but the word was stretched by a long yawn. They walked quietly from the beach, and entered their new home. The breeze made a soothing whisper as it moved through the palms. The surf maintained its faithful roll. Sleep came easily.

✿   ✿   ✿   ✿   ✿

Jane sat up in bed with a jolt! For an instant she struggled to recall where she was, and to draw from her subconscious what had alerted her. Dick was deep in sleep. Then she saw it! Or had she imagined that she saw it? Etched clearly in the moonlight, a man looked in the window directly in front of her! And then he was gone.

"Dick! Dick!" She hardly recognized her own whisper. "There's someone looking in our window!"

Dick turned. "Uhhh?" he grunted.

"Wake up!" Her insistent pokes finally roused him. Alert now, he threw his legs over the edge of the bed and stepped into the dark living room. Squinting, he tried to place the outlines of the crates and packing drums. Then he knew there was someone in the room with him!

Dick's yell escaped without warning, as a sleek figure slipped past him, sprang through the window, and off into the night.

"What happened?" Jane asked from the doorway, biting her lip to control her chattering teeth.

"Makes me feel so stupid," Dick mumbled. "Here I stood. But he was past me before I knew what was happening."

"But he's gone," Jane sighed. "Did he take anything?"

"All I saw was a blur. Let's look around and see." They lit a lamp and checked the contents of the room. "I don't miss anything. We'll know better in the morning when we have more . . . hey, wait a minute!"

"What's the matter?" Jane was obviously nervous.

"My pants! Weren't they hanging there on the corner of the wardrobe door? So that's what happened!" Dick suddenly burst into laughter.

Jane wasn't amused. "What's so funny? Bill said you have to have a sense of humor, but you don't have to overdo it."

"I can see the look on that little rogue's face when he tries to get into my size thirty-six trousers!" Dick pulled an imaginary pair of trousers higher than his head. "Where did everyone go?" He laughed again.

Jane wasn't laughing. "Those were *new* pants," she said flatly.

5. Center Avenue Comes Alive

5. Center Avenue Comes Alive

IN A FEW WEEKS, the Reed household was expanded by two: Aaron Zobad, a Kru cook from the interior, and Tom Bonoe, the watchman. As Dick moved in and out between trips to the station site, he caught snatches of Jane's instructions to Aaron.

"Now, look, Aaron, this is a *fourth* of a teaspoon. It takes two of these to make one of these." A pause. Jane was trying to make her simple instructions even more simple. "Can you tell me what this is, then?"

Aaron's laugh always preceded his answer. "I see, Missy, it's bigger, small!"

Another pause. "It's *half* a teaspoon, Aaron. It takes two of these half-teaspoons to make one teaspoon, and three of these to make one tablespoon."

Aaron tried. Jane tried. Other missionaries and other cooks were struggling all over the countryside.

One day, hungry after a tough morning at the station site, Dick arrived home for lunch. Aaron produced a bowl containing a thick, nondescript mixture. Jane's look had been peculiar when Dick arrived, and this concoction in front of him seemed to be related to the expression.

"What's this?" Dick tried to sound cheerful. "A new dish?"

"Smile, dear. You're eating your ground Spam salad sandwich, complete with onion, pickle, and salad dressing, mixed with your mushroom soup. Aaron came up with this from my poor explanation of a 'combination' lunch!"

Thousands of cement blocks were made by a simple hand-operated machine.

Construction gets underway.

There were many things to be learned about the Liberian way of life. Often the cook taught the Missy. There were new foods to prepare, using greens, palm oil, cassava, breadfruit, eddoes, or plantain. There were lessons in dickering down prices in the market, and buying fresh food at the back door.

The cook struggled to understand and learn. With patience, sometimes frayed, the Missy taught and learned. She must be freed of her kitchen routine for other impending duties.

Sick people gathered at the back door to receive help, children popped up from everywhere to watch the flannelgraph stories, and the station business demanded attention. Crates of records needed to be organized and entered on file cards.

Life in the new home settled down to a busy normal. The kerosene stove and fridge yielded to Dick's gentle coaxing. The water to be purified for drinking bubbled regularly on the stove and dripped contentedly through the stone filter. Piles of sand were brushed across the cement floors, in one door and out the other. On wash day, the splashing of water and the sound of Aaron's knuckles scraping on the washboard were accompanied by his singing of Kru songs. At spaced intervals, rogues took flight in the night as they were pursued by faithful Tom.

At the radio site, clearings were widening as dark, muscular bodies cut bush to the beat of a native drum. Picks and wheelbarrows were kept busy constructing Center Avenue.

On the corner of Center Avenue, hand-sawn native lumber lay seasoning under a thatched shelter. Irregular rows of cement blocks dried in the sun.

The three missionaries, bronzed from weeks under the tropical sun, labored, and kept the laborers laboring. They were constantly aware that with the coming of the rainy season all construction would have to stop.

They taught the Liberian workmen to mix mortar, handle trowels, lay cement blocks, and to recognize a straight line. As they supervised the building jobs, their pidgin English vocabulary increased, as did their understanding of the country people and their ways. The workmen became personalities, and finally, friends. There was warm-hearted Seabreeze, talkative Frisky Boy, and cheerful Old Man Gaminie, always snug and well-dressed in his turtleneck U. S. Navy sweater.

ELWA's first carpenter's shop was simply a work bench under the trees.

Soon the first homes were begun on the clearings hacked out near the ocean front. Trenches were chipped down the plastered walls for later-to-be-forgotten electrical outlets. Doorways and windows were set at jaunty angles, yielding to the bend of the rough, native lumber. Every corner seemed a frustrating experience of learning; the struggle with plumbing, sand and cement proportions for plastering, the difficult technique of glass-cutting, and the impatient wait for materials to arrive from the port.

At the end of Center Avenue, near the entrance gate, it was possible to plow across the high grass to the barely distinguishable road leading to the new generator house. This rectangular cement building was the first to be finished, and was now ready to house

The building takes shape.

the generator which would supply the power for the radio transmitter. The crated transmitter, two 90-foot towers, and a control console were moved inside the building, sheltered until the studio building could be finished.

At the far end of Center Avenue, the partially completed studio building stood directly in front of looming "sacred" rocks, used for many centuries as a place of pagan worship. With great fear the workmen had cleared the lot, hoping their swinging cutlasses would not disturb the evil spirits.

As Dick and Bill and Merle looked over the progress, a thrill of anticipation went through them. It had been sixteen months since the first cutlass had chopped the first brush, carving a road through the tangle to the ELWA property. Now there were the beginnings of homes, a studio, and power. It wouldn't be long, now. Not long at all!

6. God's Station Goes on the Air

ELWA mike.

6. God's Station Goes on the Air

"IT'S IN THE WRONG PLACE," Hersh Ries said. The declaration fell on Dick, Merle, and Bill like a boulder.

Hersh and his wife, Sammie, had arrived that morning, and the day had been spent showing their new technician all that had been accomplished to date. The three were pleased that they had so much ready. They thought that, once he was settled, Hersh could begin the complex installation of equipment.

But now, after studying the site, Hersh announced, "It's in the wrong place. The studio is too close to those rocks to allow for expansion. There's no room behind to work out an antenna pattern."

"But moving the studio building means moving the generator building. Or, more precisely, building a new one."

"I'm sorry, fellas, but that's the way I see it. Now, we can go right on the way things are. Get on the air faster. But we'll be tying our own hands in the process. We won't have the coverage. We won't have room to work. We won't have . . . well, the quality operation that's needed to accomplish all we are here for. You decide. You know what I think."

The decision to relocate the studio and generator building was made. With the months came slow progress. Relocation was not as easy as it seemed on the surface. Hersh was first to admit that those back in the States who were following the project, and supporting it, were weary of waiting for something to happen.

They couldn't experience the handicaps, the problems, the rain. They only knew ELWA was not yet broadcasting. Support began dropping off.

✦   ✦   ✦   ✦   ✦

No one was more aware of the support drop than Abe Thiessen. And yet encouragement came along the way. During the summer months Abe had again been a speaker at the Maranatha Bible Conference in Michigan. His enthusiasm had again caught the imagination of the guests. The specific project which the conference took was to finance the necessary diesel generator. Again, the believers at Maranatha responded, and $7,200.00 was placed at ELWA's disposal. When the generator building finally found its proper spot, the generator would be there to fill it.

It was quickly becoming evident that God had rightly designed Abe and Ellen for their part in the ELWA project. As an ambitious Canadian young man, Abe's dream had been to "make big money." And now, as a consecrated young man, it became his job to find the finances for this very big project. Aside from the building of roads and facilities, the right equipment had to be purchased and shipped. Personnel had to be recruited. Progress had to be reported. Christians had to be informed. There was a great deal to do on both sides of the ocean.

"Mister Thiessen," a man said to Abe after a meeting one night in Kansas, "the wife and I have been praying for radio for Africa for a long time. We believe you're the answer to our prayers."

The comment was typical of many. Abe's travels brought him into contact with people everywhere who shared ELWA's vision.

"That's the way it seems to be going," Abe often said, as he talked with Ellen on his return home. "God got us started doing the work, and at the same time He got a lot of people we never met praying about it. Now we come along and tell them what's happening, and they jump right in! It's like an old Christian said to me once, 'What God orders, He pays for!'"

And so they traveled, wherever they could find interested ears, telling about what God was preparing in Liberia.

It was logical for Abe to use local radio broadcasts from time to time as he spread the ELWA story. One morning, after a fifteen-minute interview, a phone call was waiting for him. The man on the other end said he'd heard the broadcast and wanted to talk with Abe as soon as possible.

That afternoon, Abe sat in the man's office. Their conversation centered around ELWA. Finally, the man rose and said, "You mentioned that you needed welding equipment."

"We sure do. We've a lot of installation to do, not to mention the tall towers."

"Come with me," the man said, and led Abe into his shop. "Take any welder you want. No charge. And I'll throw in a couple of crates of welding rods." As Abe stood, torn between amazement and gratitude, the man added, "Now, where do you want me to ship all this stuff?"

Abe stepped lightly as he left the shop. The weight of impatience, expressed by many donors, lifted temporarily. *God doesn't seem impatient*, he thought, *even if all the rest of us are.*

And God was speaking to others. In Indianapolis, Indiana, a conversation was taking place between a young businessman and his Lord. "Lord, it's clear to me what you want me to do," the young businessman said, "but you know I have to have good weather."

God had made it clear to this young man he should purchase a short wave transmitter for ELWA. His recreation park depended on good weather. The pact was made. Week after week, the hot, sultry weather brought crowds of people to the park. By fall, the young man was able to keep his $25,000.00 commitment!

In Liberia, however, the slow progress often brought impatience. The main need was a builder, a rarity on the mission field. There were new staff members to accommodate. There were studio, generator and transmitter buildings to build.

The word went out that a builder was needed. And a builder responded — Harold Dancy, an old-timer with the SIM, on extended furlough in Canada. His many years in Nigeria and Ethiopia gave him a running start.

The new studio location was chosen on Center Avenue, half-way between the old sacred rocks and the ocean. By early summer, 1953, Harold Dancy was ready to "start cracking."

The studio building's roof was up first, to protect the work below from the rains. ELWA seemed to grow before the amazed missionaries' eyes. What contrast his skill and experience offered to the eager, but amateur efforts before he arrived.

Before August, the technicians were beginning to install the broadcast equipment.

Maranatha Studio Building which housed the studios, offices and first transmitters.

Plaque in the lobby admired by one of ELWA's workman.

One year later a new wing was added to accommodate ELWA's rapid growth.

Several years later another large wing had to be added.

ELWA's continued growth as evidenced by many towers and buildings.

Still more growth takes place. ELWA Hospital is added.

Attention was now turned from building to planning program schedules as the Program Department began lining up available talent, and going about the business of radio in earnest.

Aware of the rising tide of nationalism, the staff carefully balanced the schedule between imported and African-prepared programs. Every precaution was taken to keep from becoming an American station transplanted to Africa.

On January 18, 1954, the months of hard work, disappointments, sweat, and preparation were forgotten. Three years of hard labor and detailed preparation had gone into this day. ELWA was about to begin its first broadcast.

An excited group gathered in front of the unfinished studio — the workmen, their friends and families, the missionaries and the crowd that always springs from nowhere when something unusual is happening. Seabreeze, Frisky Boy, and Old Man Gamanie were there. For months they had been told they were building a radio station. Now they wanted to see with their own eyes, and hear with their own ears that little box that talked.

In Monrovia, twelve miles away, Liberians had their radios tuned to 710 kc., waiting to hear what would result from the strange doings that had caught their curiosity over the past three years.

The crowd, now seated on the studio lawn, quieted as the voice of ELWA's big man came over the loud speaker. Mr. C. Gordon Beacham, eighteen years SIM's Field Director, now heading up ELWA, stepped to the microphone in the small, unfinished studio. A panel light flashed. The operator nodded. ELWA was on the air.

"We thank God for all that He has done to make possible this radio station with all its present equipment and staff," Mr. Beacham began. "This equipment and staff will be increased as the Lord continues to provide. We also want to thank the Government of Liberia, and President William V. S. Tubman in particular, for the grant of land on which this station stands, and for all their sympathetic cooperation. Again, we salute the people of West Africa. May God bless and keep each one of you, and we pray that every listener may know the power of salvation from sin that Jesus Christ can bring into your life.

"Let us pray. Our Father Who art in heaven, we thank Thee and praise and glorify Thy holy name for Thy great salvation brought to us in Jesus Christ our Lord. We thank Thee for establishing this radio station for the broadcasting of His Gospel. We dedicate it wholly to Thee, and pray that Thou wilt consecrate it and use it for the spiritual blessing of millions throughout Africa and other parts of the world. And grant that in that great day when Thou dost make up Thy jewels, many may be found there who have come to saving faith through the broadcasts from this station. We pray in the name and for the honor and glory of Jesus Christ our Lord. Amen."

It was a brief program but historic. It was followed up by a regular daily schedule. The studios were not completed, the towers were temporary, the schedule was limited, but the Gospel was going out.

For eight months, ELWA broadcast on a limited basis, medium wave. Four months of that was done from two rooms of the uncompleted studio building. The daily broadcasting schedule had been from 11:00 to 12:00 noon, and from 6:00 to 8:30 p.m. Often, as the announcer came to a station break or announcement he would open the studio door and yell, "Quiet!" Hammers stopped. Saws ceased. The workmen waited patiently until, "All clear!" echoed down the unfinished halls.

"If you could see all your future problems in one heap," Reuben Larson of HCJB once said, "you'd quit before you'd start." But the problems had come only one at a time.

To men like ELWA's antenna specialist, Henry Hungerpiller, with experience in the Merchant Marines, every problem became a challenge. The shortwave transmitter arrived — but what about the antenna? Henry welded together three irrigation pipes. They didn't look like much — but they did the job. Now with the shortwave transmitter, ELWA could reach outside the immediate area around Monrovia to the interior, and beyond to Nigeria.

The signal was strong and clear, even though put out at only half ELWA's potential power. The temporary 90-foot tower would soon be replaced by a permanent 240 footer. But the handicaps didn't seem to make themselves known to the listeners.

Listener response, particularly in Monrovia, was encouraging. "The broadcasts are fine and clear . . . no static!" "The variety of programs are very nice." "Oh, give me ELWA and its religious music when I am sad and lonely, blue and worried. It has always refreshed me." "I will not listen to any other station when ELWA is on."

Training in mike technique.

Training technicians.

Training in production techniques.

Broadcasts in many languages became a trademark of ELWA.

...oing out to the villages to capture the message in ...e language of the people. (Woven grass matting ...akes good acoustical material.)

Learning the many facets of broadcasting.

The letters begin to come in from listeners in many countries.

Each letter receives careful attention.

A leading editorial in the *Liberian Age,* a Monrovian daily, stated: "To join the chorus that is being sung all over the country — congratulations for the fine work ELWA is doing to spread Christianity in a nation, 93 per cent of whose citizens are in need of light and civilization."

Perhaps the most unforgettable comment in those first months came from Liberia's President Tubman. He was on his first visit to ELWA attending the dedication service for the newly completed Maranatha Studio building.

During his speech the President said, "I find the broadcasts of ELWA convincing, convicting, and converting!" Bill, Dick and Abe, who was there for his first visit, exchanged a meaningful look. Many words would be sent out in many languages from ELWA, and for many years, but there were no words to express what these one-time Wheaton student "dreamers" felt at that moment.

Before the new transmitter or antenna had gone into action, there had been many important angles for the young staff to consider. "Our listeners will no longer be just those living around here," Bill Thompson, Language Department Director, said. "We're going into the interior. There are more than twenty-eight languages used in there."

The problem is bigger than just language," Bill Watkins said. "Language is only one aspect of tribal life. They've got a whole cultural background to appeal to. We also need to know when they'd listen. When do they leave for their farms? When do they return home? Most important, *who* should speak to them on the radio? Shouldn't it be one of their own people, rather than a foreigner?"

"We'll have to prepare different programs for each different area, and broadcast them to suit their individual schedules."

"Right. *And* have someone of their own tribe handle the programs."

"That's a big order," Dick said. "But I suppose it's the only way to get the message in there."

"How many people *are* in there?" Thompson asked.

"Hard to say. The population is estimated by aerial photography of housing areas. You count the roofs and multiply by five."

"But we *are* sure of a few facts," Dick said. "We know there are twenty-eight tribal groups out there. For the most part, they are animists and fetish worshipers. They are dominated by superstition and fear. We know that their Country Devil Bush, their period of training and initiation for the boys and girls as they come of age — all that they do has a religious connotation. That's a start."

"One thing at a time," Thompson interrupted. "All these plans won't happen overnight. As the Liberians say, we'll have to 'put our foot on our heart' for that."

Erecting proper antenna to carry the vernacular programs didn't happen overnight either. As the plans took shape, so did the new towers. Henry established close rapport with the workmen. After a tedious day of clearing bush, carrying away roots and boulders, or welding the massive antenna sections, Henry and a Liberian friend would climb into their jointly owned canoe, and paddle far out into the ocean for some cool night fishing.

Days, Henry was teacher and construction engineer. The workers knew he was a friend. They also knew that when he stated a thing was to be done in just such a way, it was no use to "make palaver."

The antenna tower sections were erected by using a gin pole and hand winch. Henry's men became crack workers at rigging and greasing the guy wires. They were experts at battling the special corrosion and rust problems created by the sea spray. It was a breath-taking sight to see a workman climb the 90-foot tower with an oil can or paint bucket balanced on his head.

As the facilities expanded, so did the ministry. Seventeen missionaries were now at ELWA, and more were in preparation in the States. The first Liberian staff member was hired to serve as a typist and to study English in preparation for an announcing schedule. An order for one hundred battery radios was placed. Their destination: Liberia's interior. This was September, 1954, eight months after the first broadcasts had begun. Over $140,000.00 had been invested in ELWA.

In the homeland Abe followed every step of progress. The unique provision of the shortwave transmitter by the mid-west businessman helped him realize more than ever the importance of his part in ELWA.

"The Lord keeps me enough off balance to depend on Him," Abe told Ellen one night. "Big, important gifts of equipment, money, help, come in. The faithful little gifts — so many friends

Tower Construction.

Henry Hungerpiller and his crew surveying next job on antenna construction.

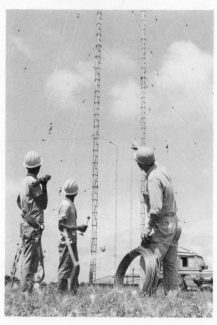

who can only give one dollar a month, and never miss. God is so obviously involved in getting ELWA on the air. And yet, just when I think we're doing a pretty great job over here, there isn't enough to pay the laborers' wages over there. And then, God steps in again, and work continues. He just won't let us forget that this is His station!"

Tower Construction.

7. The Big Voice

ELWA — "The tall preacher with the mighty voice."

7. The Big Voice

"I'M COMING . . . I'M COMING!" Herschel Ries groaned in the direction of the ringing telephone. Half awake, he threw his legs over the side of the bed and groped in the darkness for his wristwatch. Three a.m. He fumbled with the light switch. Nothing happened. That explained the ringing phone. As Technical Director, Hersh was called anytime there was a power failure.

"What is it this time?" Hersh yawned into the phone. The excited voice on the other end of the line woke him up with a start. "You mean the whole thing fell down? I didn't think the wind was that strong." More excited chatter. "Okay . . . okay. Just let me get my pants on. I'll be right over."

In a few minutes Hersh was navigating his scooter around the puddles that showed through the driving rain in his headlight. Dale Graber was standing sadly at the corner of the transmitter-generator building with a trouble light.

Hersh joined him, regarding the boards and debris strewn across the area. "That twenty-foot cooling tower doesn't look like much lying here on the ground, does it?"

"Sure doesn't."

"Good thing the generator has that automatic shut-off, or she'd be burned up by now."

The operation of the cooling tower was a vital one. A constant spray of water spilling over a twenty-foot array of boards and copper tubing into a tank below, kept the generators cool. Without this cooling system, the generating equipment, which produced the electrical power for the transmitters, would over-heat. When the tower collapsed, the automatic shut-off had stopped the power, silencing the transmitters.

"What'll we do?" Dale shrugged.

Hersh scratched his head. "Better rig up something. Let's see if we can find some garden hose."

By 5 a.m. Hersh and Dale had a small generator running with a makeshift cooling system. Water and lights were now available to the homes in Radio Village, but there was not nearly enough power for broadcasting.

A little before 6 a.m., a Monrovian housewife started the porridge cooking while waiting for ELWA's sign-on theme. Every morning her household was awakened to the cheery voice of Al Snyder on "Morning Clock." The hymns and devotional thoughts helped stabilize the family's day.

But today no sound came. She tried the dial. No ELWA. Her radio seemed to be working. But no ELWA. She slipped out her back door and up the steps to the kitchen of her nearest neighbor. Her neighbor was standing in the kitchen shaking her radio.

"My radio's spoiled," her neighbor said.

"I can't get ELWA either. It's not on the air. It will be like a friend missing."

Back at ELWA, technicians and crew had cleared away the debris. The 8000-gallon water tank was cleaned and refilled, and work was begun on a temporary cooling system in a sprinkler arrangement. Twelve hours after the damage was discovered, the big generator was operating again.

The building of the cooling system in 1959, just two years before, had been a miracle in itself. Dale and a crew of Liberians had prepared the ground for the floor of the unit. The excavation was large, and had taken two months to complete. Two tons of steel rod had been woven and tied together to fit into the excavation.

It had taken longer to prepare than they had expected, and they had been caught by the rainy season. It rained heavily day and night, but waiting for the rains to let up would mean a delay of several months. The cooling tower was needed right away.

The large floor was to be of poured concrete. That was a problem in itself, because mixing that much concrete would take machinery that ELWA did not have. And even if the concrete could be mixed, the day-and-night June rains would spoil the floor immediately.

It looked impossible. The ELWA staff prayed, and God showed them His twentieth-century power.

On a trip to Monrovia for supplies, the ELWA builder spotted a big cement mixer standing near a large construction firm. He drove up.

"Any chance to borrow or rent this thing?" he asked the foreman.

"Not a chance," the man replied. "We never let this one out of our sight. Where you from?"

"ELWA. Radio station out . . . ."

"That so?" The foreman brightened. "I was up at your place a while back. Met a guy who said he was one of the technicians. So I told him I was a ham radio operator. I been having trouble getting my set to work. He said he'd give me a hand setting up my ham rig when he had a little time." The man paused and looked from the cement mixer to the builder.

"Make you a deal," he said at last. "You guys set up my ham rig, and I'll let you use the mixer. Free."

In no time, the foreman had his ham radio rig in order. The cement mixer was delivered to the site at ELWA, complete with fifteen wheelbarrows and a vibrator to pack the cement!

But the rain kept falling. There was no sign of let-up.

Much prayer went into the problem. The staff was convinced that God was not interested in delays, and at last the decision was made.

"Get the crew together. We'll lay the floor all in one day. And we'll do it tomorrow!"

"But the rain!" the worried answers came back.

"We'll do it tomorrow," Dale asserted. "And we'll leave the rain to God."

The crew reported the following morning at 6 a.m. A cloudy and overcast sky and blackness in the south gave the usual signs of heavy rain. "It will rain for true," the Liberian workmen agreed among themselves.

Work began. The clouds grew dense. The breeze coming off the ocean became cooler, heralding the arrival of the rain. All around them the rain began to fall. Work went on. The rain was just a few hundred feet away. The attention of Liberians and missionaries alike was split between what they were doing and the approach of the rain.

"It isn't coming any closer!" someone shouted. Work halted momentarily as everyone stopped to stare. The rain was coming down in torrents just outside ELWA property, but there was only a fine mist coming in!

All day the workers poured concrete. Lightning flashed. Thunder rolled. But the rain stayed outside ELWA property! There was a strange feeling of awe among the laborers and missionaries as they laid the floor.

Late in the afternoon, the sound of a small plane turned their attention skyward. The plane buzzed ELWA and disappeared into the clouds. This was the usual signal that someone on ELWA business was landing at the airport. A car was sent to meet the plane.

At the airport Perry Draper, ELWA's diesel engineer, almost fell out of the plane in excitement. "What's going on over there?" he exclaimed. "We've been flying through rain for over 100 miles! They're getting drowned in Monrovia! But when we flew over ELWA, we couldn't believe it! Rain was falling all around you, but directly over ELWA property it was clear!"

The cement was poured by 6 p.m., and the workers left the job. A slight rain began to fall.

The technicians spent a fitful night, half sleeping, half listening. The Liberians had warned that a day without rain meant a night of flooding. But the rain did not come to ELWA. Every flash of lightning, every thunder crash brought a prayer. "Not yet, Lord. Please. Just a little longer. If it can settle tonight, tomorrow it will be all right!"

At 6 a.m. the next morning the clouds moved in and the rain broke! For three days and nights the rain drenched ELWA, a wonderful aid in curing the new cooling tower floor!

The day the twelve-ton generator equipment was to be delivered a small crowd gathered, wide-eyed at the size of the wooden crates on the back of the three trucks. The trucks plowed slowly through the mud to the new transmitter-generator building. The crates contained the elements of a 25,000-watt Fairbanks-Morse diesel generator — power enough to send ELWA's voices half-way around the world.

"Back 'er up!" Perry Draper called to the first truck driver. The truck inched toward the new board-covered cement floor.

"Hold it!" Perry's shout was mixed with frustration.

The truckbed extended several feet higher than the floor. The crate was far too heavy to lift down without a crane.

"Now what do we do?" the driver asked.

"Why not dig out under the truck?" someone ventured.

The truck was pulled away, and a slope dug in the mud. Again the big truck backed in. The surfaces matched. A cable was thrown over the crate, and a small tractor pulled the first crate onto the floor.

The process was repeated for the next, even larger box. This one held the generator motor.

"Oh, no! Look at this!" One huge unit had been packed backward in its crate. "We've got to turn this around!"

The following day the new transmitter-generator building was filled with sounds of strain and scraping as over five tons of equipment were gradually turned around inside, ready for installation.

The transmitter for which the cooling tower and big generator had been prepared had come through a series of hard-to-believe happenings. ELWA was convinced that radio beamed to Nigeria, and areas of French-speaking expression, would make significant impressions for the Gospel. The staff began praying for a 20,000-watt transmitter to be aimed toward these fields. It was a major undertaking. Back home, Abe Thiessen began making the need known.

Before long a spark of interest arrived in the form of a letter from the Foreign Missions Fellowship at Columbia Bible College in South Carolina. The group had pledged $10,000 toward the purchase of the transmitter. "This amount is impossible for us here at Columbia," the letter stated, paradoxically. "Our student body numbers only about 380, and many are working their way through school. But our eyes are not on the unfavorable circumstances, but on our unfailing Savior."

Ten thousand dollars . . . from 380 students. Certainly this was putting faith out on a limb! Each month the FMF banks were placed in the dormitories. Each month they were collected and the amount tallied. As the school year passed, some wondered if the group had bitten off a bigger financial responsibility than they could chew. More prayer went up. The money kept coming in.

Technician Dave Naff
reads the meters on 50 kw
transmitter.

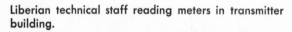

Liberian technical staff reading meters in transmitter
building.

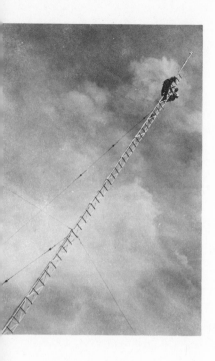

Erecting and servicing radio towers is an important and difficult task.

Australian technician Rex Vinicombe turns on the big diesel generator.

Then it was June, and deadline. The student body assembled in chapel for the final report. There was a look of awe on the faces of those who had just completed the final tally. The pledge had been met, and topped!

Sitting in the ELWA staff prayer meeting in Liberia on the morning the Columbia Bible College's gift was announced was a young American businessman. He was studying ELWA's operation with the idea of starting a radio station in Congo.

Later that day, Ray de la Haye looked up in surprise as a check floated to rest on his desk.

"What's this?" Ray asked.

"To help with the remaining amount for the 20,000-watt transmitter," the visitor announced.

The room was silent for a long time. Ray took off his glasses as though they were deceiving him. In his hand was a check for $12,000.00.

There was hardly time to react. The young man was suddenly asking eager questions. "What's the possibility of reaching out with a bigger transmitter? Could you go to 50,000 or even 100,000 watts instead?"

Ray was in partial control. "Possibilities are good, but it takes money, and lots of it. Which we don't have."

"But the Congo!" The young man was opening his heart to Ray. "Now's the time to get to that country! You could do the job with a bigger transmitter, couldn't you?"

Ray's normal careful attitude was returning. "Yes. It's certainly possible. But . . . ."

"How much more would you need to change to a 50,000-watt transmitter?" the young man burst in.

Ray studied the serious face opposite him. "About $100,000.00," he said. "Sounds impossible, doesn't it?"

"No!" the young man answered calmly. "I think I know where to find the money."

At the young man's suggestion, word was sent to Dr. Albert Helser, then General Director of the Sudan Interior Mission, asking him to find someone with entry to the New York Stock Exchange to convert his stock into cash without charging commission.

"That's easy," said Dr. Helser, but he didn't know what he was in for. No one would handle the transaction. After many futile attempts, he returned home, discouraged. "We've got to pray as we've never prayed before," he told his wife.

And as they prayed, the name of a man who might help came to Dr. Helser's mind. In a short time, the bank was forwarding the signed stock. The young man, now returned from Africa, expected the stock to bring about $85,000.00 to which he would add what was needed to bring the total to $100,000.00.

On Monday evening the stock was sent by registered air mail to Dr. Helser. A careful check of Tuesday's mail showed no stocks. Wednesday's mail was the same. And Thursday's, too.

When Dr. Helser arrived home on Thursday evening his wife placed a battered, half-opened envelope in his hand. Through the ripped end he could see the valuable papers inside.

"Look at this!" he exclaimed. "Look at this! The wrong address!" Immediately, Dr. Helser was on the phone, talking to his broker friend.

"Get them over here at once! The market is hot!"

Had the stocks arrived on Tuesday as expected, an unusual political crisis in the Near East would have affected their selling price. The market had been low. But three days later, when they *were* sold, the market was at an all-time high. Instead of the anticipated $85,000.00, the stocks brought $87,500.00!

Meanwhile, Abe Thiessen was negotiating for the actual transmitter. Disappointed by the price a sales representative gave him, Abe took advantage of being near the manufacturer and stopped in to see him.

"I'm sorry," the export manager said. "The price stands. I can't give you people any kind of break. I've got to think of my distributors."

"But," Abe said quietly, "you don't have a distributor in Liberia. So, you see, there's no one there to protect."

The export manager fumbled. "No difference. Can't give every bleeding heart a big price cut. Where'd be the business? What would happen if my distributors got wind of it?"

It was obvious that he was getting nowhere, but Abe couldn't get away from the feeling that he was here to accomplish God's business.

"Is the president of the company here?" Abe asked.

"Yes. But it won't do you any good. He'll tell you the same thing I did. We can't just go around . . . ."

"May I see him?"

In a few minutes, Abe was sitting across the desk from the president of the organization. Briefly he told the ELWA story and the need for the 50,000-watt transmitter.

"You know," the president said reflectively, "my father had a great deal of interest in missions. Used to do a lot for them."

A brief conversation and some quick calculations later, Abe strolled from the plant, a broad smile decorating his face. ELWA was going to have its transmitter . . . at a thirteen hundred dollar discount . . . with a control room console thrown in as a bonus!

And ELWA got her transmitter — in fifty-five crates delivered in seven trucks. This end-of-the-year delivery seemed to be God's final benediction on the year 1959.

All was in readiness: the new transmitter-generator for housing, trained technicians for installation, antennae for transmission and . . . potential listeners for reception.

Now ELWA's one longwave and four shortwave transmitters offered a combined power of 71,500 watts. Her voice was reaching the whole continent of Africa and beyond to the Near East, South America, and Europe.

The buildings, the towers, the equipment — all came with stories of the unique leading of God. From the start, ELWA had been God's project.

8. Aunt Clara and Others

8. Aunt Clara and Others

"AND THEN, BOYS AND GIRLS, Mr. Spider stood in front of his banana leaf house and called, 'Yoo-hoo, I'm home.'"

Inside the studio, dressed in her customary white, ELWA's Aunt Clara sat before the mike, mentally gathering her "children" about her for another Kiddies Korner program.

Jake Gargar, one of ELWA's first board operators, sat at the controls. Years ago he had been a top-notch cook. He could create a fancy pie or cook Liberian palm butter to perfection.

But one day he had said, "I can't cook forever. I'm coming to be an old man. It's time to learn a trade." Jake was becoming very conscious of the growing shiny spot on the top of his head.

"Think you can learn this?" the technician asked Jake, sitting him down before the control room board.

Jake's eyes scanned the array of knobs and dials. "Looks like an electric stove for true!"

Since that day, years ago, Jake and many Liberians have studied and become top technicians.

Jake concentrated on the voice coming through the mike in the studio. He adjusted the control knobs for a better level for Aunt Clara's voice.

"I used to be a kid myself," Clarissa Letecia Blaine-Wilson says, "with a strong will and a hard head."

It was that same will and hard head that kept her at her teacher's side at Suehn Mission School during tribal uprisings in 1916.

85

Aunt Clara and a group of her "Kiddies Korner" kiddies.

Left: The "African Challenge" program in production. Left to right: Philip Gaye, Rolen Cornelius, Eleanor Pelley, Jim Pelley, Jacob Gargar. Right: A dramatic presentation in English with Philip Gaye, Jim Pelley and Eleanor Pelley.

She was able to load and fire a rifle almost as well as the men around her.

"Bring that little girl home with you," the teacher's sister wrote from America. "She's made of the right stuff. I want to send her to school." This invitation brought little Clara to Florida. And many years later, the educated, personable young lady returned home.

The following years brought a teaching career, the founding of two schools, marriage, a son, and service to her country with the Liberian Information Service. Through the busyness and the prestige, questions kept forcing their way to her consciousness. "Why am I so dissatisfied? Why does this full life seem so empty? What am I looking for?"

As a child she accepted the gift of God's forgiveness through Jesus Christ, and had been trained in mission schools. Now, much of what she had learned as a youngster came back. "Lord, show me what's wrong. I want to serve You. Show me what's missing."

And God's will came clearly. "I have given twenty-two years of my life to government service," Aunt Clara stated. "Now I want to devote the rest of it to the work of the Lord." With these words, she retired from her post as Assistant Director of the Liberian Information Service, and joined the staff of ELWA in 1962.

Every member of ELWA's staff, African and missionary alike, is a living example of God's leading.

ELWA's Program Director, Jim Pelley, had never dreamed of radio work in Africa. In fact, it had been an anti-religious Jim who completed his professional radio training in 1950. Radio drama had been the dream of his life. Dramatics had been fun and had come easily for the young, ambitious extrovert. But radio drama was dwindling as television became more and more the attraction.

"Dear Mom," he wrote one evening after endless interviews in Boston. "No job yet. I'm so discouraged – and almost broke, too!" He looked at the words he had just put on paper, and then crumpled the letter and tossed it into the waste basket. Maybe something would turn up tomorrow.

But nothing turned up the next day. Or the next. Or the next. An old friend from radio school had stopped by and invited Jim to go with him to the Boston Garden. "Billy Graham's rallies are tremendous!" But to Jim it sounded like nothing. He begged off.

The next day his friend asked again, and Jim was too discouraged to spend the evening alone. Dr. Graham's sermon was anything but boring. And it appealed to Jim. The next night he went to the Boston Garden by himself. There, in his seat, he knew without hesitation that Jesus Christ was the One to clear up his muddy life. He walked forward with hundreds of others and accepted Christ as his Savior.

If he had been able to see the future, Jim would have been amazed to see three people in the Garden that night who would have much to do with his future. Singing in the huge choir was his future wife, Ellie, then a Bible student in a nearby school. Maintaining the broadcast equipment for the rally was future ELWA technician Ray Coddington. And singing in the Word of Life quartet was Dick Reed.

Now what? thought Jim. *Here I am. A Christian. And all I know is drama! Christians don't even* . . . . It was a frustrating dilemma.

But God had a place for Jim and his ability. "Think we might fit into your set-up out there?" Jim and Ellie had written to ELWA. In June 1958 they arrived.

As Program Director Jim's training and ability were challenged with planning, coordinating, scheduling, corresponding, trouble shooting, and producing dramatic programs. He found himself scheduling five different transmissions daily, involving forty-nine languages and a full range of program types. News, public service, government notices, public announcements, and lots of music. That was fifty per cent. The other half was Christian programming specifically — Bible teaching, preaching, drama, Bible reading, children's programming . . . everything. Liberian listeners gradually became familiar with well-known gospel programs such as Back to the Bible, Radio Bible Class, Word of Life, and Hour of Decision.

Jim Pelley couldn't do it alone. God brought others to the staff, both Liberian and missionary. All types of personalities — men like Rolen Cornelius from the State of Georgia, and Howard O. Jones from Ohio.

Rolen soon became famous for his ability to break tension with a pun or a funny story. He also simplified the complex task of scheduling the programs for all five transmissions ten weeks in advance. Working in the Traffic Department, Rolen created a board displaying rows of horizontal and parallel numbers which indicated at a glance, specific program numbers for a full week.

Aaron Vesselee "pulls traffic" in the Record and
Tape Library.

Rolen Cornelius at work in the Tape Library.

The "Corny Calculator," as it was promptly dubbed, serves as a kind of "shopping list" for the studio announcer.

With its racks of tapes and records, the record library looks very much like a supermarket. The Liberian announcer rolls out his filled "shopping basket" to the assigned studio, and, as each recording is used, he notes it on his log sheet. After sign-off, he returns the empties to the library.

American Negro Howard O. Jones quickly became known as the "Radio Pastor." Howard was a fast-rising star in the entertainment field with his own orchestra, when his girlfriend, and future wife, Wanda, was brought to Jesus Christ. On the night of her conversion she told Howard, "I believe with all my heart that God has something better in life for you, and I'm going to pray that He will break up the orchestra!"

The conflict between Howard's love for Wanda and his love for music began to show in his performance. But the public could not see the growing turmoil going on in his soul. Then, on a Sunday evening in Wanda's church, Howard was moved to acceptance of God's Great Gift.

"You know," Howard could at last agree, "I believe that somehow, somewhere, God *does* have something for me to do for Him."

Years of training and then pastoring in New York City and Cleveland followed. It was while he was a pastor in Cleveland that Howard read what turned out to be a very important article in *Christian Life* magazine. "Look at this," he pointed to the page, holding the magazine for Wanda to see. "Radio station ELWA is interested in American Negro music for use over their station in Africa." His church choir and ensembles had an audition tape in the mail soon after, and almost by return mail he received the "go ahead" to prepare weekly programs.

The program, from the beginning, seemed to work into the hearts of African listeners. Howard's preaching brought many letters of interest and numerous declarations of faith in Christ. On the strength of this unusual response, Howard and Wanda were invited to hold evangelistic meetings in Liberia, Ghana, and Nigeria. Many were led to Christ, and in 1959, when the Joneses returned as part of the Billy Graham team, again African response was warm and deep.

Howard and Wanda have moved countless African listeners with such programs as "Question Box" and "Women of Faith."

Howard and Wanda Jones in Studio 2A.

ELWA's complex ministry demands extreme care, almost a touch of genius to keep everything straight all the time. Even with the planning and cross-checking, errors are made. An error is always a source of embarrassment, but there have been times when it has been a source of excitement.

On one occasion, Mr. and Mrs. de la Haye befriended a young German who had disembarked from a ship in Monrovia, too ill to travel to his destination. He spoke no English. No one in Radio Village spoke German. His only means of communication with the ELWA staff was by gestures, smiles, and the occasional word that everyone seemed to recognize.

After rest, the young man was well enough to continue his journey. The night before leaving, he turned to his bedside radio. He was enjoying the music of Back to the Bible, even though the words were lost on him. And then, Rosella Wilson began to sing "What a Friend We Have in Jesus." She was singing in German. As he listened he was moved by the message of the song. He gave his heart to God.

Somewhere, at the same moment, a listener was saying, "What's wrong? We heard this program last night!" The Program Director was exasperated by the slip-up. Yet, there was dimension to the error. A new Christian had been born.

What programs *do* people want to hear? What will keep a listener turning his dial to ELWA? That's the question the Program Director keeps asking. One answer is "News."

"If you don't have a radio in Liberia today," one man wrote from the interior, "you're a dead man." He was trying to say he wants to know what's going on. There are many more like him. ELWA staff gives much time and attention to news.

Often the yellow Newsmobile slips out practically unnoticed to cover a local event. But one day in November, 1961, early morning activity was anything but normal as the truck whisked away. Technicians were making double checks in the transmitter and control rooms. Outside, carloads of children and staff members were starting toward town. Even the Liberian workers were dressed in their best. Everyone was "going to see the woman."

In Monrovia, at the given time, all was in readiness too.

"The gangplank is down," Al Snyder, ELWA's newscaster shouted, over the gathering crowd, into the mike in his hand. "Now the ship's officers are at the door of the yacht, saluting.

Ladies and gentlemen, this is the moment we have been waiting for. Here they come . . . Her Majesty, the Queen of England, and the Duke of Edinburgh!"

In thatched huts many miles in the interior, and in city homes all across Liberia, and beyond, listeners were sharing the cheers of the crowd and thrilling to the twenty-one-gun salute of welcome.

From ten in the morning until seven at night, ELWA covered the royal visit in the most spectacular remote set-up Radio Village had ever attempted.

Al Snyder, at Monrovia's Free Port, described the docking and disembarking of the royal couple. The broadcast switched to Arnold Lueders at the Ducor Palace Hotel, where he could see the entire motorcade route. From there, Jim Pelley picked it up at the Centennial Pavilion where the Queen laid a wreath at the Pioneer's Monument. Then to City Hall where Joseph Gbadyu was on duty.

And so it went through the day. The luncheon was described from the Executive Mansion, and the speeches of President Tubman and Queen Elizabeth were carried. The short visit to the British Embassy was followed, and finally the ride back to the *Britannia* in the harbor. The royal visit was ended.

Godfrey Talbot, BBC senior reporter, sent five transmissions from ELWA covering the Queen's visit. Two went directly to London, two to Freetown, Sierra Leone, which were recorded and forwarded to London, and one to Accra, Ghana, which was also recorded and cabled. Back in Liberia, the reports were heard on BBC's Newsreel.

As Canadian citizens, and representatives of ELWA, Mr. and Mrs. Ray de la Haye were among the 100 guests invited aboard the royal yacht and presented to the Queen and Duke. Before she sailed, Her Majesty was given a copy of *A Flame of Fire*, the biography of the SIM's founder, Rowland Bingham.

It had been a frantic, but satisfying day for the exhausted ELWA staff. Their efforts had been appreciated by the Liberian government.

"A job well done — a service to the nation," the Director of Information Services wrote.

Good news coverage involves much preparation. "We bring you now a summary of African news, compiled from the ELWA news-

Above: Control room 2 with Betty Gonkarnue and Dorothy Bollie on the job. Below: *African Observer* staff left to right: Gilberta Lueders, Bart Bliss, Sophie de la Haye, Ray de la Haye.

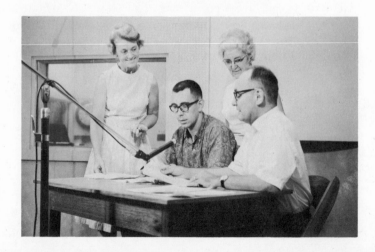

room." It sounds so simple. Few realize that the long process has its beginning in Paris.

An operator at the French Press Agency sits at his typewriter and sends the latest news of Africa in summary form, tailor-made for Liberia. At 2 a.m.: the first report for the day is handled in Liberia by a pre-set automatic switch. At 4 a.m.: a sleepy-eyed Liberian staff member receives the printed pages rolling off the teletype.

Throughout the day, a total of ten hours of news will tick through the teletype machine. These many pages of news reports must be sorted for use over the various news broadcasts. ELWA radio monitoring service, government releases, the newspaper, and the teletype supply the material for the nine daily broadcasts of African news.

Six times a day ELWA listeners hear world news relayed from the BBC.

Along with this, ten Liberian language newscasts are included on the daily broadcast schedule.

One interior listener wrote, "One time we didn't know what was going on in our own country. But now we know what is happening all around the world."

Liberia's Chief Justice Wilson discovered that one of his tribal chiefs didn't know what was going on in his own country. He permitted him no excuse.

The Chief Justice had gone interior to inaugurate the court for the newly created county of Lofa. Hundreds of tribal chiefs, required to attend the ceremony, were gathered in the little town.

After the festivities were over and the Chief Justice had returned to Monrovia, one tribal chief arrived in town.

"Everything's finished!" the people told him. "You're late too much!"

The new County Superintendent was not pleased by the lack of responsibility displayed by the tardy chief. "I say, old man, what do you mean by coming after everything is over?"

"I didn't know I should be here," the apologetic chief stammered. "No one came to tell me."

"You didn't hear it on the radio?" the impatient superintendent asked.

"No radio. How can I hear?"

"Well," barked the superintendent, "I'm not going to be sending messengers all across the country. If you're going to be a chief, you'd better get a radio so you know what's going on."

The people have come to depend on the radio. They respect the broadcasts.

A letter from the Justice Department says, "All Liberians have come to greatly appreciate the great Christian and social services which Radio Station ELWA renders to the Republic of Liberia, so that today when one speaks of the Republic of Liberia, one's mind runs simultaneously to the various reports which are made over Radio Station ELWA from Liberia. This is indeed a great achievement for any radio station, for this proves that the public has learned to repose its confidence in those responsible for the operation."

Confidence in the public service offered by the radio station has resulted in confidence in the spiritual message of ELWA.

9. The Many Feet of Radio

Rev. Perry Draper searches
the Word of God to an-
swer listener questions.

9. The Many Feet of Radio

A YOUNG CHRISTIAN TRIBAL PRINCE in Ghana struggled alone with his thoughts. "Now that I'm a Christian, how can I ascend to my father's throne? Juju . . . sacrifices . . . many wives. How can I do it?" He needed the answer and who would understand? He wrote an urgent plea to ELWA for help. "I know that a Christian cannot practice juju, as I will be called upon to do as a ruler. I am afraid I will lose my soul if I partake in this pagan activity forced upon me by the tradition and law. Shall I be an ardent king, or abdicate and be a follower of Christ?"

In Sierra Leone a young, educated husband leaned against a mango tree thinking deep thoughts he could not share with either of his wives. Lines etching his face gave indication of his deep concern. Which way to turn? By the light of the kerosene lamp he started a letter: "Dear Radio Pastor: Do I commit adultery if I keep two wives, or should I divorce one even though neither has offended me?"

❖ ❖ ❖ ❖ ❖

Miles away at Radio Station ELWA in Liberia, Perry Draper looked over the stack of letters on his desk. "These are tough ones to answer," he said, half aloud.

As Director of ELWA's Counseling Department, Perry finds that the most difficult questions have a way of ending on his desk. He and his assistant Don Miller, though seminary trained and with rich

backgrounds of practical experience, often feel helpless to un-
tangle the complexities spelled out for their counsel.

Common questions regarding tithing, drinking, church attend-
ance, and overcoming temptation have answers found in the Question and Answer file, neatly alphabetized and cross-referenced.

Booklets and pamphlets and other helpful materials on such
topics as juju, charms, country medicine, secret societies, dowries,
lotteries, and bribery, as well as materials with spiritual insight
in the areas of Christian growth are sent to those who express need.

In 1954, the letters were easily handled by one missionary.
There were about twenty-five each week. But as ELWA sounded
out all over West Africa, the letter response mushroomed. Perry
and Don now channel nearly 25,000 letters, one quarter of ELWA's
100,000 annual letter response, through the missionary and Liberian
workers who round out this department.

A letter addressed to the Counseling Department puts ELWA's
long-range plan of follow-up into motion.

For salvation: Three separate letters urging definite decision.
For instruction: Five letters at spaced intervals explaining basic
truths of the Christian faith. For growth: An introduction to
SIM's monthly magazine, *African Challenge,* Navigator's memory
course, Scripture Union's daily devotions, and an introductory Radio
Bible School course. For encouragement: Semi-annual letters and
literature from ELWA's Radio Pastor to English-speaking listeners.

The 60,000 Radio Bible School students are found everywhere
across Africa. Some study in the quietness of their home or school.
Others pore over the Word of God in prison cells or behind palace
walls.

The need of Gladys Nyako, educated, attractive daughter of a
Ghanaian Paramount Chief, led her over many miles to the door
of prophets and spiritualists. The cost was dear — physically, emo-
tionally, and financially.

"Where can I find it?" Gladys asked her friend. "Peace of mind,
peace of heart . . . peace of soul?"

Gladys had found useless the powders, medicines, good luck
ring, and incantations of the spiritualist. Ringing in her memory
was the prediction of the prophet: "You will become sick and
die in a lunatic asylum."

"*I* found peace," her friend assured her. "Study this Bible course
and see."

Gladys read the opening pages. "Stop trying to find peace by yourself. Try peace in Jesus Christ." Hungrily she devoured the truths of the Bible course. In Jesus Christ she found the peace for which she was searching.

It was a peaceful Gladys who volunteered her spare time to ELWA's Bible School branch office in Kumasi, Ghana. And it was a grateful, dedicated Gladys who later graduated from Toronto Bible College, prepared now to lead others to the One who gave her peace.

Many Africans are searching for peace, but not finding it in their old superstitions.

"What shall I do? Temptations are around me and are hard to resist," a Gola man from the far interior of Liberia writes. "My grandmother and mother believe in juju. As a Christian believer, I can't believe or practice it. Please pray so the Lord can change their minds and save them."

This letter is passed along to the Gola Broadcast Director, Kpakala Dabeh. Kpakala will answer the man's letter and send him literature in his own Gola language. And here is a question for him to answer on his Question and Answer program prepared at ELWA and beamed to his own people back in the hinterland.

Kpakala Dabeh had come a long, hard trail to ELWA. He had prayed for several years that God would let him preach in the little "box that talks," but the way was always barred.

As a young man, living deep in the heart of the Gola forest, Kpakala was an affirmed animist and fetish worshiper. Along with the other young adults in his village, he attended the Country Bush Society School to be trained and ultimately initiated into the Gola tribe. His father was a Country Society leader, and Kpakala often watched as he appeased the gods deep in the sacred forest with food or chicken sacrifices.

Then missionaries came. They came with a story of a God who loved the Gola people enough to die for them. It was a strange thing for a God to do. But it captured the attention of the village. Some believed.

Kpakala was frightened at the change in his father. One day the smoke of burning fetishes filled the air. His father resigned from the Country Society. There were no more trips into the sacred forest. His father explained his new life, and the day

Kpakala watched his father being baptized, he, too, accepted Jesus Christ.

From the start, Kpakala burned to tell his people of the new freedom he and his father shared. He seemed to know that education was essential. Month after month, he studied at the mission school. Finally he found himself sought after as a translator.

In Monrovia, working with the American Bible Society, Kpakala saw a strange and wonderful thing. The missionary had a small box which, at the push of a button, could fill the room with Gola preaching! "Who is that Gola man talking in the little box? How did he get there? Who feeds him?"

As simply as possible, it was explained to Kpakala that he was listening to a Gola gospel recording, being played a few miles away at ELWA. Proudly, the young Gola man carried a "little box" back to his people.

"Some day I will preach in the little box," Kpakala told his fellow villagers. But each time he requested a place on the ELWA staff, the answer was the same: "You must have eight years of school. You must know English so that you can read the Bible. You must study."

"You will never work there!" his neighbors laughed. "They only want 'book' people at ELWA." But Kpakala kept praying, kept asking, and kept being refused.

Then, as if to shatter all his hopes, a young friend of Kpakala, a high school graduate, was hired to fill the position of ELWA's Gola Broadcaster. "Let me come, too," Kpakala begged. "I want to learn books and help with broadcasts!"

"All right," the answer came. "You can come. But your friend must be responsible for you and help with your English." A delighted Kpakala had his foot inside the ELWA door.

Then plans changed. The friend never reached the station. Kpakala arrived alone. He was hesitant, afraid he might not be allowed to stay. But God had obviously brought him, and he was welcomed.

In spite of his age and his "one-one" English, Kpakala proudly sat every afternoon in the second grade class in Radio Village School. His mornings were spent in preparing Gola programs and answering mail. Kpakala broke the rules because God wanted him there. He was Gola Broadcast Director long before he finished the eight years of English school he "had to have."

"Things are not like they used to be among the Gola people," the missionary who first preached to Kpakala's people states. "Since ELWA came, many Golas are coming to Christ through the broadcasts."

God has led other men like Kpakala to ELWA to carry on as Language Broadcast Directors.

Edwin Kayea had come, unannounced, dusty and certain that God wanted him to be the voice of his Gio people. He had traveled many miles by foot and truck, and the strength in his round, black eyes commanded attention.

As the grandson of a Paramount Chief, and the son of a Clan Chief, both devout Muslims, Edwin had spent his early years in a Koranic school. His perceptive questions about the Koranic verses he wrote only brought shrugs from the untrained malams who were his teachers. "Walk straight," they said, but he could see no example of this advice in their living.

Later, as a student in the nearby Worldwide Evangelization Crusade school, he saw the missionaries living what they preached. With deep repentance for his wasted years, Edwin turned to Jesus Christ, and the peace he had been looking for filled him.

"Grandfather, I have renounced my Islamic faith."

The words seemed to draw the life out of his grandfather. For a long time, the old man sat, without speaking. His favorite grandson had become an apostate.

The invisible wall that formed between Edwin and his family was felt, if not seen. He was avoided. No longer was he one of them. His school funds were stopped. His friends turned their backs when he approached. He was an outcast. And no one cared about his new faith in Christ. "They won't even listen!" he prayed to his Lord. "How can I tell them?"

For ten years Edwin lived with this pressure. His mother was despondent when she learned he would marry only one wife. Tradition allowed him four, and as many concubines as he pleased. But only one! His mother's anticipated relief from her household labors would not be realized.

One evening, as he lay near an open window, absorbed in thought, *a terrible-wonderful thing happened.* Bright jabs of lightning began to dance in the sky, casting eerie shadows through the room. Suddenly, a blaze of fire streaked through the window, blasting mercilessly over Edwin's body. The blinding light, the awareness of fire near his head, the echoing of shattered glass, the awful stench, the sense of being propelled through space by some unseen power — all followed each other in unreal succession. He sank as though sucked into a whirlpool of blackness. Somewhere, seemingly many miles away, his mother was shouting, "He's dead! He's dead!"

Edwin was aware that time had passed. How much, he did not know. He opened his eyes and forced them to focus. A small, anxious group of neighbors was gathered around his bed, staring down at him. His mother was touching his limp form, and repeating, afraid of the answer, "My son, you are not dead? You are alive?"

There was a celebration that evening. The family who had rejected him for ten years suddenly rejoiced that he was alive.

"Come, my boy," his grandfather smiled. "There is a man here who has the power to make medicine so that you will never be troubled by lightning again!"

Edwin's face fell. Here was more warmth and love than he had known from his family since becoming a Christian. But to refuse the services of the medicine man, retained by his now-loving grandfather, could shatter it all. "Lord," Edwin prayed silently but in desperation, "give me the words!"

There was a pause as his grandfather waited for Edwin's reply. Then the words came. "Grandfather, if God could keep me yesterday, He'll be able to keep me tomorrow."

The old man considered the words for a moment, then snapped his fingers and the medicine man was dismissed.

From that day on, those who had turned their backs began to listen as Edwin spoke of Jesus. Some months later, his father said, "I believe you have the truth." And later his mother stated, "My son, the road you carry, I must carry."

During these days as Edwin listened to English and Liberian-dialect programs coming from ELWA, he began to feel a deep tug at his heart. "My Gio people must hear of Jesus in our language." Unable to push this desire aside, and confident that it was the prodding of God, Edwin made his way to ELWA. In due time he became Broadcast Director for the Gio language programs.

ELWA's shortwave broadcasts make it possible for Liberia's interior people to sit under a palm or mango tree and hear the Word of God in their own language on transistor radios.

"It takes me a long time to cross rivers and mountains to get to a village to talk about Jesus," one national pastor said, "but now when I finally get there, the radio is already in the place talking. I only have two feet, but radio has many feet."

An evangelist, walking from village to village to preach, said, "Every time I used to blow my horn to call people to church, only a few people would come. Now I put my radio on the table and tune in the Gio requests. So many people come now it looks like a market place! When the Gio program is finished, I shut off the radio and preach to all the village!"

Placing transistor sets in villages all across the country has become a favorite part of the language men's work. Equipped with recording gear, the men travel up-country. At times they walk several days through the bush to interior places to record music and messages in their local language for broadcasting at a future date.

ELWA now has more than two thousand pre-tuned radios distributed throughout Liberia, Sierra Leone, Ivory Coast and Guinea in hospitals, prisons, schools, orphanages, private homes, and villages.

"More than sixty people listen to my radio," says one Christian pastor who proudly cares for an ELWA radio. This "box that talks," costing about $25.00, is his to care for and to keep tuned to ELWA.

Kru fisherman Peter Denuh found his way to Radio Village. He had a story to tell and he wanted everyone to hear it.

In his home at River Cess, along the sea, he fished for a living. At times ELWA's Kru Broadcast Director, K. T. Bessman, would come to preach.

"That man," Peter said, "he talked about Jesus and it humbugged me too much. When he come there, I get vexed and go on the beach or out to sea. Sometimes a missionary would come to our town to preach. But he only scratched the ground with his preaching. He didn't cut down the trees."

But Peter couldn't get away from God. A woman in his town

Edwin Kayea editing tapes
in the news room.

Transistor radio in Northern Nigerian village with
people listening to Hausa,
broadcasts beamed from
ELWA.

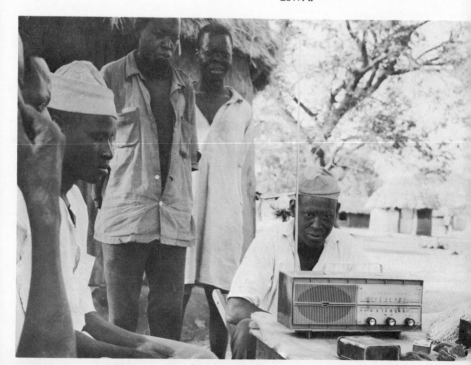

A portable Missionary Radio does its work in a Liberian village bringing the Gospel to the people in their own language.

Blind evangelist and students can hear God's Word through an ELWA radio in Kano, Northern Nigeria.

A PMR placed with a leprosy patient, shares its message with village children.

got a radio. She called all the Kru people to hear K. T. Bessman preach the Word of God. Peter listened, day after day, but he didn't like it. What would he do with his three wives? And what would he do with his sugarcane juice drinking?

"I say," Peter's grin reached from ear to ear, "this man preaching on the radio filled my bucket full and running over. I got saved!"

And Peter's friends could see the difference. He left his old ways and followed Christ. "I want to go to Bible school now and go back to my town and tell them about Jesus."

As one young man from the interior put it, "The drum has been replaced by the radio."

Africans tune to ELWA's
many broadcasts.

10. Remote Recording Studios

Pastor Ba'ako records Hausa messages in the ELWA-
Jos Studio, Nigeria.

10. Remote Recording Studios

It was July, 1960. Two men at the Uganda airport appeared visibly relieved as the jet lifted from the ground. Their two hundred Congo Swahili tapes were safely on their way to ELWA at last.

Independence . . . rebels . . . unrest . . . it all figured into the picture. But so did God.

God's timing had allowed the two Baptist missionaries to complete a recording trip throughout the vast Swahili area just before rebels swept in. His timing made possible the bringing of the completed tapes across Congo's border before they closed. And now they were on their way to Liberia, to be broadcast and beamed right back to the Congo.

One of the speakers on the tapes would soon be a martyr, killed by the rebels because of his stand for Christ. But his voice would live after him, sending the message of God's love and forgiveness to thousands of listeners across his native land.

About the same time as the set left the Uganda airport, in Luluabourg, Congo, missionary Charles Sprunger viewed his mission station from a Missionary Aviation Fellowship plane. The rebels hadn't left much.

Not long before had been "a red letter day" for Charles. After months of working and sweating, building and equipping, training and recording, the first programs in the Tshiluba language were ready for ELWA. But now he looked down at the total destruction below and shook his head in disbelief.

Bill Thompson checks a point with national pastor Falla Bimba of Liberia.

A group of Gospel Singers from the Krahn tribe of Liberia record in Moore Memorial Studio.

Bill and Betty Thompson working out schedules with national staff Samuel Tabalow and Jacob Gargar.

Back in Liberia, ELWA waited patiently for the promised box of Tshiluba tapes. Nothing came. Months passed. Then came a letter from Sprunger, postmarked "U.S.A."

Charles had been through something. The rebels had moved into Luluabourg and through his studio. After a thirty-mile march at sword-point, Charles had been carried to safety by a U.N. plane. But the rebels had left their mark. The new studio — burned. Equipment and tapes — destroyed. Sound truck used only a few times — smashed. Total destruction. The whole set-up — lost. Everything lost except Sprunger's determination to reach Tshilubas for Christ.

Another letter from Sprunger — 1965. Postmarked "Luluabourg, Congo." Another box of tapes — Tshiluba. Another studio — built and equipped in Luluabourg. Another start — expanded now to supply daily programs to reach the four and a half million Tshilubas.

During the Congo crisis, long-time missionary William Baerg reluctantly left his Lingala people to return to his home in Manitoba, Canada.

"If ever the Lingalas needed Christ, it's now," he said. At home, with the blessing and support of his church, Baerg kept preaching to the Lingalas in the Congo. His taped programs were sent to ELWA, and beamed on to Congo.

In 1964, eager to locate and broadcast in Congo. Mr. Baerg began an extensive tour. From Leopoldville to the depths of the interior he asked everyone he met, "Do you listen to ELWA?"

"We *do* — it's the only church we have left"; "How could we get along without it?" "All the time," came the answers.

Later that year the Baergs returned again to the Congo. With the help of Christian nationals, programs were soon being prepared in his studio in Leopoldville (now named Kinshasa). With the flick of a radio dial, five million of Congo's thirteen million Lingalas can be reached.

In a chicken coop is where Congo missionary Willys Braun began taping programs. This time it was the Kikongo dialect. "If the chickens don't complain," he wrote, "neither will I."

With a vision — and little else — he began the programs reaching the three and a half million Kikongos via radio. The chicken coop served its purpose until the construction of a new studio.

Missionaries from many denominations are working in twenty-five ELWA-related remote recording studios in Nigeria, Ivory Coast,

Jonathan Shea, missionary technician, and class of potential radio technicians.

Al Snyder instructs a group of youthful African announcers.

A new shipment of Portable Missionary Radios from Holland.

A Hausa Orchestra is recorded for ELWA's musical programs.

Sierra Leone, Ghana, Mali, Lebanon, Congo, and Brazil. They tape sermons, Bible readings, interviews, news, programs of interest to the local people.

These tapes are sent to ELWA, and beamed back to their target areas. Broadcasts in forty-nine languages go to the entire continent of Africa, the Middle East, South America, and beyond.

Joyce Flint at SIM's remote studio in Igbaja, Nigeria, turns out tapes like an assembly line, taking advantage of the fact that the studio is on the campus of Igbaja Theological Seminary. Students help write, record, and produce the Yoruba programs.

"I nearly lost my soul when I contacted a fetish priest for healing," one young educated Nigerian wrote to her. "But your programs helped turn my mind."

A Hausa listener responded to the message given by one of his own people. "I'm here to tell you the fullness of my 'white stomach' (joy) when you talked about believing in Christ. It was as though you poured cold water on my heart."

"If a man listened to that program very much," a pagan writes, "he would have to give up his sins."

New advances, new languages . . . encouragement and discouragement. This is the story of the remote studio ministry.

"You can preach to us for 100 years," one Muslim told a missionary couple in Guinea years ago, "but you will never convert us to Christ."

But he didn't figure on modern radio with the voice teaching the Word of God day by day in the homes and villages, where Muslims could listen in privacy.

"The Muslims tell us about religion," one Muslim government official recently told this same couple, "but it's you people who get us straight with God."

11. Broadcasting in French

11. Broadcasting in French

SINCE THE DEDICATION IN 1958 of ELWA's strongest voice, the 50,-000-watt shortwave transmitter, ELWA's broadcasts have included French, one of Africa's major languages.

Ninety million French-speaking Africans, that's what ELWA's energetic French Broadcast Director Max Weber, from Switzerland, considers to be his parish.

They were his parish before he joined ELWA staff — back in the days when he traveled thousands of miles every year through West Africa holding conferences, Bible studies, showing films, and distributing literature. But he was only one man.

In 1958 Pastor Weber, his wife, Jacqueline, their twins, and a new baby girl arrived at Radio Village. At the time, the French broadcasting from ELWA was limited to a few programs prepared in the U. S. and Canada, with virtually no follow-up being done.

In two months, the Webers had added to the sparse shelves of French tapes the complete New Testament without comment, plus Psalms, Proverbs, Job, and twenty-four children's programs.

Soon afterward Max and his family joined ELWA, and the French Language Department really came to life.

"Having heard your address on the radio, I am writing to know the answer to many vital questions about Jesus Christ, our Saviour," a typical letter from a listener starts, and is followed by half a dozen specific questions. From the start the broadcasts and correspondence were too much for one man to handle. Max

Max Weber of Switzerland
directs French broadcasts
to Africa.

A new shipment of Radio Bible courses in French is
opened by Simon Koudjrako, Moustapha Seidou and
Pastor Weber.

never took a correspondent lightly, and most of the personal letters resulted in much consideration, prayer, and a chain of correspondence.

The French Department quickly grew to a staff of nine workers, four of them French-speaking African Christians.

Of the more than 14,000 enrolled in the fourteen French Radio Bible courses, one man's story stands out. Almost without exception, when a student completes one Bible course, he enrolls in the next. But this young man, in prison in Cameroon, made a strange request: "Please send me the whole series of your lessons so I will not have to wait between courses."

The young prisoner, Jacques, had been the rebellious son of a preacher of the Gospel. He had done everything possible to displease his parents. He longed to leave home. To live. He cringed every time his father would say, "Jacques, I know God will make you a preacher some day."

Finally, he was away from home. He was living the way he wanted, free from the binding standards and regulations of home. And then it happened, so fast that Jacques could hardly believe what his anger had done. The body of his victim had dropped at his feet. The witnesses were all around him. Suddenly he was in prison . . . for life!

He wrote to Max at ELWA. With all the time in the world to think, he changed his outlook. He asked for a Bible study course, the whole series at once. His lessons and New Testament were like bread for the hungry. As he read the Word of God, and prayed, Jesus Christ became real. His life was changed. He was still in prison, but everything was different.

As time passed, the content of Jacques' letters to Max changed. "Yesterday I was able to take down the name of the twenty-sixth convert since my illness in the hospital. Two of them are Muslims. I was so happy I wept for joy! I am so happy that God is working through me. Indeed, what could I do without Him? It is He who calls His sheep. What a joy to see them come to Him. There is so much to do here. Pastor Weber, each evening I remember you and your station in prayer. I am united to you in the Lord."

It was 1965, and Jacques was stretched across his cot, reading.

"Jacques," the guard called as his keys jangled in the lock. "The Commandant wants to see you."

In the office, Jacques stood before the Prison Registrar and the

Commandant, both followers of Islam. On the desk was an opened letter with the return address of ELWA in the corner.

"Who is this man, Pastor Weber, who has written this long sermon to you, comparing Christianity with our religion?" the Commandant asked, arching a curious brow. "Why does he think lightly of Islam?"

"This man is a shepherd of the true and living God," Jacques said, with surprising freedom. "He is not making light of Islam. He is saying that Christianity is the true way to God."

For half an hour Jacques spoke with the prison officials, referring them to the Scriptures.

The two listened with undisguised interest. Finally, the Commandant said, "I am now giving you permission to have the radio Mr. Weber has offered to you."

"Radio, sir? What radio?"

The letter was handed to Jacques. Pastor Weber was offering him a radio. And the prison would grant the permission.

Jacques was ecstatic! In gratitude, he offered his New Testament to the officials. They accepted, but a small warning was issued. "Do not speak to anyone about what has happened here. When we discover the truth ourselves, we will write to this shepherd of yours."

12. The Medicine Man Cometh

President Tubman signs guest book.

12. The Medicine Man Cometh

"FOR 12 YEARS we have been listening to your Christian programs," Liberia's President William V. S. Tubman said at ELWA's hospital dedication in December, 1965. "But now we are going to see you put into practice what you have been talking about."

A tour through the modern 26-bed hospital was visual evidence that the "practice" was already set into motion.

"It all started by a mistake," Dr. G. Christian Weiss, Back to the Bible's Director of Missions, said concerning ELWA's new hospital.

In 1960 an extensive trip took Weiss to Monrovia, Liberia, for an over-night stay. A mixed-up schedule extended his visit. During those days God placed a burden upon his heart: Radio Village needed a hospital. Back to the Bible could help.

This wasn't the first thought for a hospital at ELWA. Since the beginning, every knock on the back door bringing a frantic mother with a child bitten by a snake, or a nervous man pleading for help for a wife in labor, turned the minds of the missionaries to the need of a hospital.

"We did the best we could with our medical kits," the early missionaries recalled. "But what did we know about yaws, dysentery, amoeba, malaria, and delivering babies? Too often those needing help had to be turned away."

But the ELWA staff wasn't satisfied to turn the needy away. They began to pray.

ELWA Hospital with car at main entrance.

Telephoto shot of ELWA Hospital taken from a radio
tower. Atlantic Ocean in background.

Before long, word of the gentle nursing at ELWA was spreading around the countryside. Increasing numbers of people from neighboring villages were coming for treatment.

"I need a clinic," nurse Bea Barnard said. "It doesn't have to be fancy."

It wasn't. There was no money for a new construction at ELWA. The work on a new studio building was slow. But the materials were there, and with a little imagination, a clinic was put up. Building blocks were stacked for the walls. They couldn't be mortared because they would ultimately become the walls of the new studio. Asbestos roofing sheets were placed across the top, and the new clinic was finished.

It wasn't fancy, but it worked. And as more Liberians came and were treated by the nurse and received the Word of God, and as missionaries and their children were saved miles and hours when they were ill, the need for developing and expanding this service became more obvious.

Local mothers saw how babies delivered at the clinic survived, and they began coming to ELWA for help. A mid-wife was added to the staff.

Pre-natal care and instruction were among the first major projects undertaken by the nurses. Many times a country woman in the last stages of a complicated delivery was brought to the clinic after there was little hope. The stuffing of leaves to stop bleeding had brought infection, a mother weakened from loss of blood was unable to deliver, or some complication made a normal delivery impossible. Gradually, the care and instruction began cutting away ignorance and tradition.

But often the nurses were faced with diagnosis and treatment beyond their training. They prayed for a doctor at ELWA.

God began to speak to individuals around the world concerning their part in the medical picture of ELWA.

In Michigan, a young doctor in his second year of surgical residency wrote a letter to ELWA. His question: "Are you looking for a doctor?"

The letter arrived just before the West African Field Council meeting of the Sudan Interior Mission, where official approval was given for the ELWA Hospital.

"God is answering our prayers," Dick Reed announced to the staff at prayer meeting one morning. "Back to the Bible Broadcast

has felt led of God to present the ELWA Hospital as their Project
of the Month. They are trusting God to provide $10,000.00 for the
first hospital wing."

A month later the good news came. The goal had been reached.
Back to the Bible was sending the $10,000.00! The money repre-
sented gifts from listeners all across the United States. But that
wasn't all. A few months later Back to the Bible forwarded
another $10,000.00, this time from a farmer as proceeds from the
sale of his farm.

But perhaps the most unusual donation, which also was channeled through Back to the Bible, came from a small town in Texas.
First, a check for $10,000.00 arrived, designated for the hospital
building. A few weeks later, another check came from the same
person for $5,000.00. This second check had a simple message
attached: "To help equip the wing and building for my people
in Liberia."

A few months later, Abe and Ellen Thiessen were in Houston,
Texas, and made it a point to drive to the small town of Edna to
find the generous donor. There she was, at the edge of town, in
an unpretentious white frame cottage. They met a small, stooped
Negro lady of almost ninety years of age. The surroundings and this
unimposing little figure gave no clue as to her ability to produce
$15,000.00 as she had done.

When Mrs. Josephine Carmichael was told that Abe and Ellen
were from ELWA, she was animated with excitement. A recent
hurricane had damaged the house, and it was under repair, she
told them. "But if you'll just wait here on the porch, I'll fetch my
sister, and a little something to refresh yourselves."

Mrs. Carmichael's sister, Ophelia, was also excited by the visitors,
and hurried faster than her ninety-some years usually allowed. It
was from Ophelia that the unusual story of the donation began.

"Grandfather and father were slaves. Grandfather had been
brought here from Liberia. I don't remember from which tribe.
I don't know as he ever told us.

"I've always wanted to help our people in Liberia. I even tried
to be a missionary at one time. That was back in 1925. I guess
being over fifty years of age at the time was against me. I got sick
and had to come back."

"We've been Christians since we were young," Mrs. Carmichael
picked up the story. "I married late in life. I'm afraid Mr.

Dr. Schindler directs tour of Hospital facilities during dedication. Left to right: Dick Reed, Secretary of State Grimes, President Tubman, Dr. Schindler.

Dr. Schindler introduces President Tubman to Chief Nurse Karen McLain at Hospital Dedication. Dr. Barclay, Director of National Public Health Service, and Secretary of State Grimes look on.

Dr. Robert S. Schindler, Director of ELWA Hospital.

Carmichael wasn't all he should have been. He made a lot of money buying land, and more land. He didn't spend his money very wisely. Well, when he died, I decided to use his money for the Lord. It's been since 1953 that I've sent money here and there to Christian causes.

"Then one day I was listening to the Back to the Bible program, and they told about you wanting to build a hospital out there in Liberia. I wrote to them for some more information, and when I found out about you . . . well, I sent that little donation."

Abe was present in Liberia at the Hospital Dedication, as was President Tubman. Abe told the story of his visit to Mrs. Carmichael. President Tubman responded immediately. "I want that lady to visit Liberia," he said. "She'll be our guest at the Executive Mansion."

Since health would not allow her to travel so far, the Liberian Ambassador in Washington, His Excellency S. Edward Peale, flew to Texas. It was a big day in the little town of Edna. The band was out, the citizens, Abe and Ellen Thiessen, Aunt Clara, the mayor . . . all to see one of Liberia's highest decorations, Knight Commander of the Humane Order of African Redemption, conferred upon Mrs. Carmichael.

Building ELWA's hospital required more than a man with just medical training. It demanded aggressive compassion. In the enthusiastic Dr. Robert Schindler, God found the right man.

Even as a child Bob talked of being a doctor some day. He was born into a Christian home in Berne, Indiana. His pre-med training began at Wheaton College in 1948, but while serving on the Word of Life Camp staff, his sights were definitely set for medical missions.

He met and married Marian Wilson, Taylor University graduate from South Dakota. In the fall of 1962, God brought the Schindlers, together with their two boys, to Liberia to begin the hospital project.

A second doctor, Dr. Robert Bowers, shares the load at the ELWA Hospital today. The second "Dr. Bob," with his wife — also coincidentally Marion — came as an answer to prayer. Schindler's furlough was due, and a replacement was urgent.

All Liberia had been "home" to Bob. He was born of missionary parents serving in the interior of Liberia.

From the beginning — as far back as he can remember — his one

Karen McLain, Chief Nurse at ELWA Hospital, instructs future Nurses' Aides.

Historic photo shows Dr. G. Christian Weiss (center) conversing with Ray de la Haye and Dick Reed. It was at this time that the idea of the ELWA Hospital was first suggested.

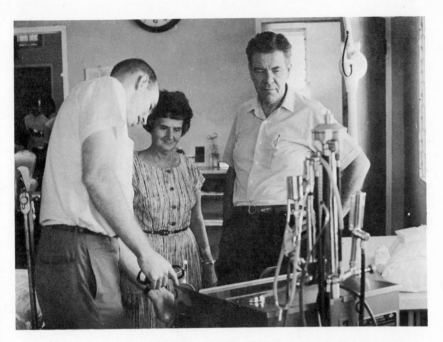

Dr. Bowers conducts S.I.M. General Director, Ray Davis, and his wife, Evelyn on a tour of ELWA Hospital.

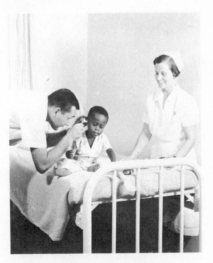

Dr. Schindler examines child in Pediatric Ward, while Nurse Mary Hollingsead stands by.

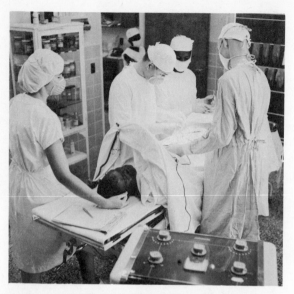

Doctors Schindler and Bowers operate while Nurse-Anesthetist Ruth Bliss does her important work.

Liberian RNs Marie Moustapha and Alice Lankah ably assist Dr. Schindler during surgery at ELWA Hospital.

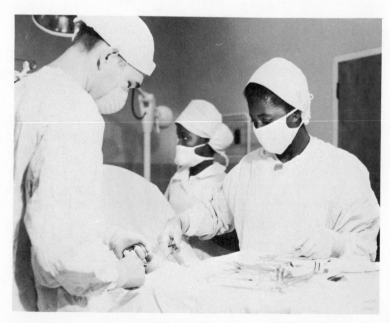

thought was to be a missionary doctor. The years piled up: pre-med at Wheaton, Baylor University Medical School, marriage to Marion Lacey from Pennsylvania, and then together, God's place — Liberia.

Staff provisions continued: a hospital administrator expelled from the Sudan, a dentist from Egypt to double as Arabic preacher, a nurse anesthetist, a lab technologist, an X-ray technician, and a dedicated group of missionary and Liberian registered nurses and aides.

Every piece of equipment is a story in itself, often a sacrificial story. The specialized lab equipment, new X-ray machine, anesthesia machine, the gleaming sterilizer — all give evidence to a modern hospital in Africa.

At Duke University Medical Center in the United States, six thousand miles away, modern medical missions is demonstrated in action. A little gadget hooked to the new electrocardiogram machine in Liberia converts heart tracings to electronic impulses. These are transmitted via ham radio, fed into a computer, studied at Duke University, and the interpretation relayed via ham radio back to Liberia.

ELWA Hospital serves Liberians from every walk of life, from tiny tetanus babies from the "bush" up to high government officials. Each receives the same expert care from the Christian doctors and their staff.

The Christianity put-in-action to which President Tubman referred, works hand in hand with the gospel programs heard over ELWA. With the twist of the dial, each patient can turn his tiny pillow receiver to a program in his own language.

But there's no substitute for the gentle, loving care and spirit of Christ displayed by the staff.

There's the mother of twins, the first set born at the ELWA Hospital, who told her people, "I born twins at ELWA Hospital, and I was born again."

And little Gabriel, with his twisted back. He had TB of the spine. But over 100 miles up-country his people were aware of the Christian love and care he received. They turned from their witchcraft and the worship of water to faith in Christ.

An old chief tried to drink poison to end his life. The pain and despair from suffering with an ugly leg ulcer was too much to bear. Surgery and spiritual encouragement helped him leave with a renewed faith in God.

There is little Moustapha, the first tetanus baby, brought to the clinic by his tall Muslim mother. The recovery of this little fellow opened up a hard Muslim village for a Bible class.

But a special little baby in the noisy row of bassinets perhaps best represents the ELWA Hospital, the need, and the sacrifice of others for the sake of Christ.

This special baby, expressing herself with the universal yowl, is alive today because ELWA missionaries gave her life. She'll be going home with a grateful mother, and will open up in her village opportunities for the same missionaries to offer eternal life.

"A few days ago," the doctors could tell you, "that newborn baby was dying from RH incompatibility of the blood. The only hope was to completely replace her blood with new blood. Staff members donated their blood. The exchange literally gave her life."

Which, of course, is a beautiful symbol of what ELWA is all about.

13. Right Around Home

Anita Draper teaches first and second grades at
ELWA Academy.

13. Right Around Home

"FIRE! FIRE!" THE SHOUTS shattered the peaceful Sunday morning air. Radio Village came alive with activity. Fire had broken out in the small three-room apartment used for station guests, and as temporary quarters for new ELWA staff.

It was a freak fire. Some clothes, stacked in the closet, had toppled onto the light bulb which had been left burning to help keep the closet dry. The heat had caused a can of fly spray to explode. By the time the fire was discovered the whole interior of the apartment was burned out.

It was over in a few minutes, but the damage had been done before the fire was discovered. On the ground lay a charred sewing machine, typewriter, luggage, projector, smoldering mattresses . . . everything the newly arrived missionary couple opened — ruined.

The new couple reacted quietly. They took graciously this sudden "spoiling of their goods."

Most of the "spoiling" ELWA missionaries learn to live with is gradual.

To live on the ocean's edge is a complicated business. There's no stopping the salt spray, humidity, and corrosion.

Radio equipment is kept on most of the day, even when it isn't in use. The heat helps keep dampness and subsequent rust and corrosion under control. A special de-humidified "dry closet" is used to store spare parts. Tapes are kept in a dry atmosphere.

Every twenty-four hours one gallon of water is pulled out of the record library air to keep the zinc oxide from softening on the tapes, and to keep records from warping.

The missionary homemaker joins the struggle, too. Her best efforts seem useless: waxing, scraping, painting, protective plastic coating. Few materials resist the attacks of mold, rust, fungus, or mildew.

When a pink plastic shower curtain became peppered with black mildew, one missionary, deciding to "join them because he couldn't lick them," sent home for a black replacement. But in time, the black curtain produced mildew too, this time in white!

To keep up a house can seem a time-consuming, insurmountable task. Along with constant corrosion comes the battle against salt spray on windows, sand from the beach, red laterite dust in dry season, and 240 inches of rain in the wet season.

A busy schedule complicates the problems. There's little time to polish and pamper. The missionary woman doubles as a script writer, typist, bookkeeper, musician, teacher, or nurse. When she leaves the house at 7:30 a.m. for staff prayer meeting, she's not likely to be back home until noon.

Help in the house has become part of the overall picture at ELWA.

Simple? Yes and no. At any rate, it's necessary. But it takes time and patience to convey to someone unskilled in modern ways the million-and-one household routines a woman has learned over many years. In the process she is constantly driven to maintain a sense of humor: the ability to laugh when a plastic dish is found melted in the oven, or when work is done half-way – perhaps not at all.

For nationals having known a simple, carefree way of life, the imported ways are strange. The "different-different" foods take a long time to fix. And then there's the "Missy" who talks too fast and expects everyone to work at the same pace she does.

One Liberian lad fresh from up-country and new at the "kitchen palaver" was cooking breakfast for the first time for a missionary couple. At chop time back in his village he put one big pot of rice on the fire and then sat down and watched it cook. But now he had to keep *two* pots cooking at the same time; one with coffee and the other with porridge. And while the two pots cooked he had to slice bread, and put dishes on the table.

He did his best. Finally he leaned against the wall and mopped his brow. "Missy," he said, "in my country, one man can't roast two rats!"

Today, with changing times, it's not unusual to see a Liberian teenager living with a missionary family. Helping in a house makes way for studying at Radio Village School.

Afternoon classes at the school offer opportunity for every Liberian employed at Radio Village, regardless of age, to attend school. The Liberian teachers, following the Department of Education curriculum, conduct classes for men, women, boys and girls, ranging in age from thirteen to thirty.

Some students continue with high school after graduation. Each day several ELWA staff members are dropped off at the University of Liberia, in Monrovia, where morning classes balance afternoon jobs at ELWA. A scholarship program is available to needy students. The final product is a developing staff of competent, educated Liberians.

Important station positions of announcing, broadcasting, typing, teaching, or assisting in the medical work are filled by ELWA's "kitchen graduates."

Reliable, trained househelp and a smooth-running household aren't the final answers to a new missionary's problems of adjustment. Learning to live with co-workers is sometimes another.

Missionaries are real people with real problems. They're ambitious. They get bored. They get discouraged. They get angry, frustrated, just like everyone else.

In a small, closed community such as a mission station everyone knows the hours you work, the hours you sleep, where you go, who comes to see you. Missionaries see each other for what they really are.

It's understandable that missionaries get to know each other well, sometimes too well, living, working, playing, socializing, praying — everything with the same group of people.

Here is where character and spiritual qualities really count. One Liberian cook told his friend: "For two years I worked for those missionaries, and never once heard a cross word between them." And then he added, "The husband always let the woman have her way."

Disappointments vary. One missionary expressed it this way: "I thought missionary life would be talking to Africans day after day about Christ. Not so. For a long time I didn't feel like a missionary. Work in the studio, behind a desk, organizing technical things and social affairs . . ."

The "work." There's so much to do — and so few to do it.

The temptation comes to work and work to the neglect of prayer and Bible study.

One hard-working missionary found that he was dissatisfied and critical. Blessing was somehow withheld — until he took the time to get back into fellowship with God. Then he understood his problem. "When I got too busy with the 'work' to pray and read my Bible, then my troubles began."

The problems of working together are real, but the problems are small compared to the satisfaction and joy the missionaries at ELWA experience. They work together in true team spirit with harmony and friendship.

Early morning music and laughter comes from the Nursery School where thirty children, national and foreign, between the ages of two and four are having morning stories, songs, and games.

Kindergarten is taught by a qualified teacher, to prepare Liberian and missionary children for first grade.

The silence of hard work surrounds ELWA Academy where fifty students study. The Academy has five large classrooms, a well-equipped library, and good recreation facilities. The staff offers missionary children and Liberians a sound educational and spiritual foundation.

After speaking at a young people's group in America, one ELWA missionary's child concluded, "Life in Liberia is exciting. I love it. I'd much rather be a missionary kid in Liberia than just an ordinary American boy." But he admitted he missed the corner hobby shop with its supply of model cars.

Taken all together, living and working at ELWA is a complex, wonderful life. A satisfying life. A life with the God-given task of reaching the entire continent of Africa . . . the Middle East . . . South America . . . and beyond with the Gospel.

That's why ELWA missionaries can't forget that God made everything happen. They can't forget every miracle that put up every tower, that brought each missionary and Liberian staff member to Liberia. God did it.

14. Assignment: North and East

14. Assignment: North and East

THE MIDDLE EAST AIRLINES jet thundered through the skies high above the Nile River Delta. Absorbed in deep thought, Raymond J. Davis, General Director of the Sudan Interior Mission, was unaware of the passengers around him. But he was aware of the nagging feeling which kept alive his sense of deep disappointment.

It had only been a few minutes since he had sought out a quiet corner of the Cairo airport, as excited as a little boy with a new toy. The toy was his transistor radio. He had moved the dial up and down with a great deal of anticipation. *Here I am,* he thought, *right in the middle of a stronghold of Islam, and ELWA is beaming the message of Jesus Christ straight this way!*

He moved the dial again. There it was! The Arabic broadcast! Loud and clear; as strong as a local station. It was even better than Dr. Davis had expected. But at the station break, his heart dropped. It wasn't ELWA at all. It was the Voice of Islam. Nasser's powerful 900,000-watt transmitters were dominating the dial.

Dr. Davis worked the dial. At last he found ELWA. It faded. There it was again . . . and gone again. It was there, all right, for anyone with the patience to keep after it. But there were lots of places on the dial where the Voice of Islam boomed out without hesitation.

The loud speaker at the Cairo airport had called him back to his plane. It was here that he sat, strapped in his seat, the weight of the many Muslim millions on his heart like a great stone.

145

Dr. Zarifa opens the Word of God and proclaims the truth of the Scriptures in Arabic.

Arabic broadcasters convene at ELWA. Bassam Madany of "The Hour of Reformation" on the left. Dr. Suhail Zarifa, Arabic preacher-dentist, on the right.

"Oh, Lord," he groaned, "what can we do?"

"The radios are here," God seemed to be saying. "The Voice Islam is powerful day and night. Does not the Gospel merit a voice as strong and accessible?"

"Of course, Lord," Dr. Davis almost spoke aloud. "But theirs is supported by a government. It's terribly costly."

"You think I don't know that?" God seemed to smile, much as Jesus must have smiled at the small faith of those who had seen Him do so many miracles. "Ask Me . . . and I will give it to you!"

Dr. Davis opened his eyes. The sunlight pouring through the small window of the airline was almost blinding as the plane rose above the clouds.

Back in 1958, ELWA's outreach to the Islamic world had started small. A weekly fifteen-minute Arabic program, Saat ul Islah (The Hour of Reformation), was begun with an enthusiastic Bassam Madany at the microphone. The program was beamed toward the Sudan and Southern Arabia on ELWA's 10,000-watt transmitter. In two years, only three letters came to the station as a result of the program.

"Preaching to Muslims is the last thing I would ever have chosen to do," Bassam would say. "As a child back in Souedea, Syria, I knew God wanted me to be a missionary. I told him to send me to Japan or China — but not to Muslims. They were impossible. They had conquered our forefathers. How could I go with a message they dislike?"

As a young man, Bassam took further training in the United States. "When I first heard of ELWA, I couldn't believe there could be a radio station to reach Arabs."

Late in 1960, with the support of the Back to God Hour, Bassam's daily broadcast began over ELWA, aimed at the entire Middle East by the new 50,000-watt transmitter. Within a year, 473 letters came from many parts of the Arab world, especially along the Nile in Egypt.

As the response grew, and as the newly vigorous effort of Islam to win Africa gained in strength, ELWA saw its history taking a new turn.

Able men and women began to make themselves known. New recording studios started supplying ELWA with tapes from Beirut and Marseilles. ELWA broadcasts to the Islamic world began going out in Arabic and French, meeting Muslims where they live.

No one is more aware of the growth of Islam in recent years than the ELWA staff. The Supreme Islamic Council, headquartered in Cairo with its Al Azhar University, is training and sending out hundreds of missionaries a year.

Radio, as well as literature, has been stepped up to a dizzying pace under Nasser's rule. His dream of a Pan-Islamic political empire is more than an impractical vision. It is being pushed.

A news release issued by the King of Morocco has left its impact. "It is. not possible to conceive of an African unity outside the framework of Islam. If Africa wishes to play the role which is its due in accordance with its wealth and importance, it must be united. And this unity must be built around Islam."

"They're dead serious," Dick Reed said to Bassam Madany, visiting ELWA for a special Arabic Conference. "They're saying, 'In heaven there is Allah and on earth there is Nasser.' They're a pretty powerful team."

"Our team is powerful, too," Bassam said. "With the Beirut Studio in Lebanon, the North Africa Mission staff at Marseilles, and Suhail Zarifa right here at ELWA . . . and Someone more powerful than all the rulers of earth."

"Knowing Muslims as you do," Dick said, "where do you begin in presenting the Gospel to them? Creation?"

"We begin with the human predicament. We're all in the same boat, sinners needing a Savior," Bassam said. "When a Muslim hears an Arab preaching in his own language, he can't help but be impressed at the redemptive character of the Gospel compared to his own legalistic faith."

ELWA's Arabic Conference underlined three things in connection with the Arabic broadcasts: The aim — to present the Word of God in a relevant way. Present program output — inadequate to meet present need. Expansion — increase in facilities, power and broadcast hours absolutely necessary.

The addition of Suhail Zarifa to ELWA's Arabic staff put wings on program production. Back in Gaza, Palestine, he had listened to the broadcasts, and had vaguely wondered if somehow, someday, he might be able to help.

In 1959 after an Egyptian theological student introduced Suhail to Christ, God's plans for him unfolded quickly: completion of dental training at the University of Alexandria, immigration to Canada, studies at Vancouver Bible Institute, contact with the Sudan

Interior Mission, candidate school — and then to ELWA with a combined dental-Arabic broadcast ministry.

Suhail shares the outlook of a veteran missionary with the North Africa Mission.

"There are signs of progress and change everywhere in these ancient and exotic places. Not the least remarkable evidence of these changes is the omnipresent transistor radio. No family appears too poor or isolated to have one. The transistor radio has become the status symbol of the Arab world. It is not unusual to hear the sounds of radio coming from the back of a donkey, from the midst of a desert caravan, or from a Bedouin tent.

"Places previously closed to Christian witness are now open to the voice of God. Each new transistor radio becomes a prospective missionary for Jesus Christ. Gospel broadcasting is new in the lands of Islam. It is captivating and arouses curiosity. It presents, logically and systematically, the claims of Christ. Most important, it is private. A person can listen to the radio without stigma or public intimidation."

After months of prayerful planning, ELWA formulated a plan for expansion: "Assignment: North and East." It will involve many physical changes in Radio Village, many new faces, and many continuing miracles to see it through.

Four miles from ELWA property, 300 acres of land have been surveyed and stand ready for ELWA use. One Liberian Christian lady has *given* fifty acres to the work of God. The land will ultimately hold an entirely new antenna system, a larger transmitter building, a new power station, and other service buildings.

"Assignment: North and East" will also include two new transmitters to blanket North Africa and the Middle East with the message of Christ in Arabic, English and French.

"This program of expansion," Dick Reed told the West Africa Council of the Sudan Interior Mission, "will permit an enlarged schedule and greater signal strength for the broadcasts beamed to the populous land of Nigeria, and to the broadcasts in the French language beamed out to West and Central Africa. These are the areas in which Islam is making its greatest advances today, the areas of greatest conflict between the Prophet of Allah and the Christ of God."

As in the past, those whom God has placed in leadership of ELWA are anxious to move, anxious to see how much and how quickly the challenge can be met.

"Every day," Dick says impatiently, "we hear from some listener. Look at this letter. 'I was born a Muslim. My father was a very strong leader of the Islamic religion. I have been educated in the Islamic school in Iran, and was previously a strong believer in the faith of Mohammed. Thanks be to the pastors of ELWA. It has made me make a decision. Having put Christ and Mohammed on the scale, oh, I took Christ as my Savior. My daily listening to ELWA has made me put away all my chickens, kola nuts, sheep, and other sacrifices, and take the Bible to be my guide.'

"That's the kind of man who's out there by the millions! He needs more than a weak signal as his message from the living God!" Dick concluded.

In the United States, Abe Thiessen got busy. He located a new, 50,000-watt transmitter, exactly the type needed for the expansion program. It was already partially paid for. "You can have it for the remainder of the bill," the manufacturer told him. "The company that ordered it went bankrupt before they'd paid the thing off. Works out to be about twenty per cent discount."

❖   ❖   ❖   ❖   ❖

When the transmitter arrived at the end of 1967, Dick and Jane Reed with other staff members gathered to see the off-loaded crates. The night air was cool as the Reeds walked home along the beach. The slanting sun reflected on the glistening whitecaps breaking across the expanse of ocean.

It had been sixteen years since they first arrived in Liberia. ELWA then had been the dream of a few college kids. It was still a dream — an expanded dream, with unbelievable potential.

They stopped, and looked out across the rolling surf. "You know," Jane said, at last, "over there in the States they're saying that God is dead."

Dick tossed a pebble into the waves. "I know," he replied. "But it's a good thing we didn't know that back at Wheaton when all this got started."

They walked toward the house, the hum of the diesel generators in the distance, and the tall steel towers rising into the darkening sky.

The Reed family 1967.

The housing area on the ELWA beach.